PICTURES OF ISLAM

MERCER
UNIVERSITY PRESS

Endowed by
TOM WATSON BROWN
and
THE WATSON-BROWN FOUNDATION, INC.

PICTURES OF ISLAM

☪

Donald Lee Berry

Mercer University Press
Macon, Georgia

MUP/P370

© 2007 Mercer University Press
1400 Coleman Avenue
Macon, Georgia 31207
All rights reserved

First Edition.

Books published by Mercer University Press are printed on acid free
paper that meets the requirements of American National Standard for
Information Sciences—Permanence of Paper for Printed Library
Materials.

Library of Congress Cataloging-in-Publication Data

CIP data are available from the Library of Congress

To my wife Carolyn

CONTENTS

Preface   ix

Introduction   1

Chapter 1: A Picture of Pre-Islamic Arabia   6

Chapter 2: A Picture of the Prophet Muhammad   17

Chapter 3: A Picture of the Qur'an   35

Chapter 4: A Picture of Islamic Groups   57

Chapter 5: A Picture of Islamic History   72

Chapter 6: A Picture of Muslim Law and Life   86

Chapter 7: A Picture of Islam and Modernity   99

Chapter 8: A Picture of Contemporary Islam   114

Chapter 9: A Picture of Islam in Praxis   136

Chapter 10: A Picture of Muslim-Christian Relations   146

Bibliography   165

Index   171

PREFACE

Pictures of Islam

Why do we need another book on Islam? Although numerous excellent books on Islam have been written, I have noticed that many popular introductions lack the depth needed to understand more than the basics of Islam. The academic books written on the subject provide an excellent source of information, but they are not written for a general audience. My intent was to write an introduction providing both depth and readability.

Since the horrible events of September 11, 2001, the media has been providing Americans with bits and pieces of Islam. Much of the material presented on television or in the newspapers either lacks accuracy or does not provide an adequate context to help the audience understand the unity and diversity within Islam. Much of what I see and hear in the media and from individuals has done nothing but promote certain stereotypes of Muslims that may or may not be applicable to all Muslims.

I will try to present several different pictures that provide a mosaic of Islam. The first chapter offers an introduction to the cultural environment of Arabia from which Islam emerged. The second chapter contains a biographical sketch of Muhamad, who, according to Islam, received the final written revelaion given by God. The third chapter offers the reader a glimpse of the basic teachings found in the Qur'an, the sacred writing of all Muslims.

Chapter 4 provides a survey of important groups within Islam that allow diversity in the midst of unity. Chapter 5 enables the reader to learn of significant historical events and movements that have shaped contemporary Islam. The sixth chapter addresses the development and implementation of Islamic law. Chapter 7 focuses on the dilemmas of modernity for Islamic communities around the world. Chapter 8 addresses the key issues facing contemporary Islam. The ninth chapter deals with the everyday lives of Muslims as they seek piety and a sense of community. Chapter 10 is about Muslims and Christians. The final chapter focuses on Muslin-Christian relations. My hope is that the reader can see beyond the stereotypical descriptions of Muslims portrayed by the media since September 11, 2001.

Clarification of Terms

Throughout the book, the reader will encounter italicized words that represent Arabic terms that will be transliterated in the text. A transliteration is a word that captures the sound of the original language written in the letters understood by another language. In short, Arabic sounds will be written in Latin letters used by an English-speaking audience. Muslims use a dating system that recognizes the year A.D. 622, when Muhammad journeyed to Medina, as the starting point of their calendar. All years after the journey to Medina are designated as AH, and the years prior to the journey are designated BH. The Muslim calendar also uses a lunar calendar, meaning a month consists of the completion of the four phases of the moon. Thus, the Muslim year has 354 days per year, whereas the Gregorian calendar has 365.25. Over time, every important Muslim celebration will take place in each of the four seasons of the year. Since the Muslim year is several days shorter than the Western calendar, dating events can be an interesting challenge. Because the audience of this book primarily uses the Gregorian calendar, I will date events using *Anno Domini* (A.D.).

Some common Islamic terms need to be clarified. *Islam* refers to the religion, while *Muslim* refers to a person who practices the religion. Islam means submission to God, and a Muslim is one who submits to the will of God. *Allah* is the Arabic name for God. The prophet who was instrumental in establishing Islam in Arabia was *Muhammad*. The religion should never be referred to as Muhammadism. The Scripture revealed to Muhammad is called the *Qur'an*. Alternative spellings such as *Mohammad* or *Koran* have been replaced by *Muhammad* and *Qur'an* to reflect a more accurate rendering of the Arabic terms. *Shi'ite*, however, may still commonly appear as *Shia* or *Shi'i*.

I hope that you will find this book helpful.

Don Berry

Author's note: All dates are A.D. unless otherwise noted.

INTRODUCTION

Islam has existed since the seventh century, but the events of September 11, 2001, have caused millions of Americans to seek an understanding of the religion associated with those who perpetrated acts of terrorism. This book provides an introduction to Islam that aims to help the reader understand the diverse Muslim populations worldwide and deal with current events involving Muslims that continue to dominate the media. The Gulf War, acts of terrorism, continued encounters with Osama bin Laden, and the Israeli-Palestinian conflict have all brought the religion of Islam to the attention of people around the world. Many have asked the question, "Are these events and personalities representative of all Muslims around the world?" This work was written to provide information that will allow readers to respond to this question.

Islam as a world religion began in Arabia but is now represented in most countries throughout the world. More than one billion people identify themselves as Muslim, which makes it the second largest religion in the world after Christianity. According to the Institute of Islamic Information and Education, the largest Muslim population is found in Indonesia.[1] Below is a list of the top twenty-five Muslim populations around the world according to the institute. The populations are rounded off to the nearest million.

---

[1] http://www.iiie.net/node/65.

Indonesia, 216 Million

Pakistan, 161 Million

India, 147 Million

Bangladesh, 130 Million

Egypt, 74 Million

Turkey, 70 Million

Nigeria, 66 Million

China, 53 Million

Iran, 67 Million

Ethiopia, 35 Million

Algeria, 32 Million

Morocco, 33 Million

Sudan, 29 Million

Afghanistan, 31 Million

Iraq, 26 Million

Uzbekistan, 24 Million

Saudi Arabia, 27 Million

Tanzania, 19 Million

Syria, 16 Million

Yemen, 21 Million

Russia, 18 Million

Malaysia, 10 Million

Senegal, 11 Million

Tunisia, 10 Million

Seven countries with 7 Million or more (Azerbaijen 7,
Burkino-Faso 8, Guinea 8, Kazakstan 7, Kenya 7,
Niger 8, and the United States 7)

This list demonstrates that most Muslims are not located
in the Middle East. Muslims around the world are linguistically
and ethnically diverse. Readers should also note that most
Muslims do not speak Arabic as their mother tongue. In fact,
most Muslims do not speak Arabic, although most can recite
portions of the Qur'an in Arabic.

Muslim populations in Europe have risen to more than
twelve million through immigration, biological growth, and
conversions. According to the Institute, Austria, Bosnia-Herze-
govina, Bulgaria, France, Germany, Romania, Russia, United
Kingdom, and Yugoslavia all have more than one million
Muslims each. Mosques and Islamic centers can be found
throughout Europe. Although many of the Muslims emigrated
from former colonies (Pakistan, India, etc.), many of the recent
arrivals have come from war-torn areas around the world.

Islam is currently listed as the fastest-growing religion in
the United States. The changing of immigration laws in the
United States in the mid-1960s has opened the door for non-
Europeans to immigrate to the United States. The influx of
immigrants, biological growth, and conversions has resulted in
the quadrupling of the U.S. Muslim population in the last
thirty years. The United States is home to more than 1,200
mosques, and more than half of them have been established in
the last twenty years. Today, Muslims in the United States
outnumber Episcopalians, Lutherans, Presbyterians, the
United Church of Christ, and many other Christian
denominations. In order, the ten states with the largest Muslim

populations are California, New York, Illinois, New Jersey, Indiana, Michigan, Virginia, Texas, Ohio, and Maryland.[2] Abdul Malik Mujahid suggests that the United States has 200 Muslim schools, about 500 Sunday Islamic schools, and six schools of Islamic higher education.[3] Muslims in the United States serve in the professions of medicine, engineering, computer science, education, and hundreds of others, representing a true cross-section of American occupations.

Today, Islam is in a period of transition. Muslim radical groups like al-Qaeda are making news because of their strong anti-American rhetoric, while other Muslims are trying to become good citizens of the United States. Although the radical groups seem to dominate the headlines, groups like the Center for the Study of Islam and Democracy (CSID) receive little attention.[4] My hope is that this book will provide a context that enables the reader to gain an understanding of the diverse population of people who call themselves Muslim.

C*

The title of the book is called *Pictures of Islam*. The reader may be surprised to find no pictures of Bedouin or of the Qur'an in

---

[2] Council on American Islamic Relations, 2000. http://www.cair-net.org/pdf/American_Muslim_Voter_Survey_2006/.pdf

[3] Islamic Information & Products, http://soundvision.com. http://www.soundvision.com/info/yearinreview/2000/profile.asp.

[4] CSID is a Washington, D.C., Islamic organization that desires to address the recent trends of Muslim radicals who see themselves as the "defenders of Islam."

this volume, but one must understand that Muslims create pictures in words rather than through photographs. The goal of this book is to present several snapshots of Muslim history, teaching, and practice to create a mosaic of the world of Islam.

Chapter 1

A PICTURE OF
PRE-ISLAMIC ARABIA

In order to understand Islam, one must first understand the context of Muhammad's birth. Pre-Islamic Arabia was a land of contrasts. One could find extended families moving from place to place searching for grazing land for their sheep, goats, and camels. One can imagine movable tent communities, much like those of the Bedouin people of today, which would journey from one watering hole to another. Yet, one could also discover urbanites who had developed a thriving trading business with nearby communities.

Pre-Islamic Nomadic Life

The social fabric of pre-Islamic Arab society was the tribal system. Every Arab was a member of a tribe that consisted of smaller groups called clans. Each clan was composed of numerous extended families. Tribal identity motivated members to live and, if necessary, die for the tribe. The survival of the tribe and the protection of the tribe were of ultimate importance. Loyalty to the tribe was essential in order for the tribe to grow strong and withstand any conflict with outside tribes. The honor of the tribe as a whole and the honor of any member of the tribe had to be protected. If any threat came from outside the tribe, it was met with the united force of the tribe so that the tribe could survive against all opposition. Any threats from within the tribe were dealt with swiftly so as not to threaten tribal unity. One must remember that life in the desert was harsh, requiring everyone to do their part for the group to survive. The only relative comparison in American history would be the days of the early settlements, when nobles and commoners were forced to work together for the survival of colonies such as Jamestown.

Arabian culture was patriarchal, so one's tribal identity was traced through the male. Tribal pride and male pride were highly valued in pre-Islamic Arabia. Men could marry as many wives as they could afford, and having many sons was seen as a sign of virility. Conversely, having many daughters was often viewed as a lack of virility. The pressure of proving one's manliness led to a detestable practice called infanticide. Sometimes when a female child was born, she would be quietly taken out during the night and killed. The community would be told that the child was born dead. This practice ensured the protection of the man's honor.

Women had few if any rights in pre-Islamic Arabia. A woman received no portion of her father's inheritance and had no choice of whom she would marry. The father or other related male representative typically arranged a daughter's marriage. A woman was under the authority of her father until she married, and then, as she was considered weak and in need of a man's protection, she came under the authority of her husband. All rights related to marriage and divorce belonged to the males in pre-Islamic Arabia. For example, a man could divorce his wife by the thrice pronouncement "I divorce you, I divorce you, I divorce you."

The political fabric of Arab society focused on the tribal and clan leaders. These men represented the voice of the tribe or clan. Decisions made by tribal leaders were binding on all those within the tribe. The clan leaders had the same level of authority within their clans. The tribal and clan leaders functioned as judges, arbiters, and models. Because they lived an egalitarian life, the leaders exercised great authority, yet they lived a lifestyle similar to that of their people. An example of the influence of the clan leader is evident in Muhammad's life. The leader of Muhammad's clan, Abu Talib, was also Muhammad's uncle. Abu Talib used his position as clan leader to protect Muhammad when he began proclaiming his first messages from Allah to an unreceptive audience.

Because tribal identity was so important in pre-Islamic Arabia, conformity to strict guidelines within the tribe was essential, but behavior toward those outside the tribe varied greatly depending on the relationship between the tribes. Combined with the importance of honor, this way of life produced inevitable conflict. Because tribal identity was so important and the good of the tribe must be defended at all costs, feuds developed between tribes. When one tribe somehow dishonored or harmed another tribe, the result was almost assuredly retaliation. The law of the land suggested that justice demanded comparable compensation. Without some standard of fair compensation, feuds were common between tribes and even occasionally between clans of the same tribe. The closest parallel in American history is the famous feud between the Hatfields and McCoys in eastern Kentucky. If a Hatfield shot and killed a McCoy, then someone from the McCoy family was expected to avenge the death by killing a Hatfield. Without the influence of an outside mediator, one can imagine how the situation would escalate into a full-blown feud. Feuds were a common part of pre-Islamic Arabian life.

The economic fabric of the nomads depended on animal husbandry. Camels were especially important because they served many different functions. At times when water was scarce, camel's milk provided life-saving liquid. Camel skins were used to make tents, camel meat provided food, and camels offered the most reliable source of transportation because they could handle the dry, sandy environment of Arabia. The dung from the camel was dried and used as fuel for fires. The animal was used as the bride price paid to the bride's father to compensate the family for the loss of a family member. Today, small jewelry boxes made from camel bone still exist in the Middle East. The camel was also used by raiding parties that attacked villages or caravans to provide goods for the benefit of the tribe, although when a fast-moving animal was required, the Arabian horse became another valuable commodity.

Some Arabs offered themselves as mercenaries who were hired to fight in battle or to protect the caravans from possible raiding parties. Capturing individuals from rival areas and selling or using them as slaves was another source of income. To provide meat for the people's diets, hunting of wild game was also an important part of Islamic life. The various fabrics of nomadic life in Arabia wove a tapestry that was male dominated, demanding, and emphasized the importance of family duty and loyalty.

Pre-Islamic Urban Life

Another picture of Arabia prior to Muhammad's birth was the developing cities. The cities grew as a result of the trading generated by caravans traveling along the western coast of Arabia. Caravans needed places to obtain goods and collect water. The cities of Mecca and Medina (*Yathrib* in Arabic) had developed to provide for the needs of caravans. The reader should note that Syria and Iraq did not exist in Arabia in the sixth century Pre-Islamic Arabia included parts of territories that today belong to Syria, Iraq, and Kuwait. The northern part of Arabia connected with the major trade routes of the day. Besides animals, Arabia produced some of the most expensive spices in the Near East. Frankincense was a fragrance made from the white resin of trees around the Dhofar region and, according to Christian tradition, was brought by Balthasar, one of the wise men who gave a gift to the infant Jesus in Bethlehem. Incense was also made from the same resin. Myrrh, another well-known fragrance from Arabia, was made from a yellow-orange tree resin. Spices such as cinnamon and cassia were also used for trade with countries around the Mediterranean. Arab cities emerged as persons shifted from herding animals to the trading of goods. Cities became the gathering place of merchants seeking to trade their goods. The trading of spices, gold, and slaves were important to the Arabian economy.

Although many areas had holy sites that were the destination of pilgrims, the city of Mecca was especially dependent upon the pilgrims who traveled there as part of a spiritual pilgrimage. As many as 360 deities could be worshipped at the famous Ka'ba, and pilgrims could also drink from the famed Zam Zam well. According to Arab tradition,

Hagar and Ishmael found this life-saving spring after being expelled from the camp of Abraham. Caring for the needs of the religious pilgrims became an important part of the Meccan economy. The polytheism of the time allowed Mecca to offer pilgrims the opportunity to honor one or more deities in one location by providing them all the necessary amenities related to their journey.

Another part of the Arab economic life was the practice of usury. Goods or monies were lent to individuals, and they were expected to pay back two or three times the initial loan value. Although the lines between the rich and poor were relatively small among the nomadic peoples, the result of this practice in cities like Medina meant that a few individuals maintained economic power while the others were destined for poverty. The gap between the wealthy and the poor was clearly observable in urban Arab life.

Arab Heritage

Arabs are genetically and linguistically Semitic. The term *Semite* refers to those who are descendants of Shem, one of Noah's sons who survived the flood recorded in Genesis 7 in the Christian and Hebrew Bibles. The Bible describes Abraham as a descendant of Noah's son Shem, thus genetically any descendant of Abraham can rightfully be called Semitic. Because of this, both Jewish and Arab people claim to be heirs of Abraham, which means both can use genetic evidence to refer to themselves as Semitic. Some Arab tribes trace their genetic lineage to Abraham, who is featured in the biblical book of Genesis. Some of these tribes trace their lineage to Abraham through his son Ishmael, who was born to Abraham's maidservant Hagar. According to Islamic tradition, Hagar and

Ishmael became the first residents of Mecca after drinking from the life-saving waters of the Zam Zam well. Other tribes trace their lineage to Abraham through his wife Keturah. According to Genesis 26, after Abraham's wife Sarah died, he married a woman named Keturah and had several sons. Those tribes that trace a direct lineage to Abraham through Ishmael or Keturah live in what is today Jordan and Iraq. Although the terms Semitic and anti-Semitic are used commonly by the Jewish community, at least some Arab tribes are genetically Semitic.

Arabs are also Semitic through their language. Arabic is a member of the Semitic language family that includes Hebrew, Syriac, Ethiopian, Aramaic, and others. Many Hebrew words used in the Bible are similar or even the same as the Arabic words used in the Qur'an. The word for prophet in Hebrew and Arabic is *nabi*. Many people are familiar with *shalom*, the Hebrew word for peace. The word comes from the root *s-l-m*. In Arabic the word for peace is *salim*, which has the same root, *s-l-m*. From that root, the words *Islam* and *Muslim* are formed. *Islam* means to submit to God or to do the will of God faithfully. The term *Muslim* refers to one who submits to the will of God. The term *nephesh* in Hebrew and the Arabic term *nafs* both can be translated soul or living being. The Hebrew word for daughter is *bat* and the Arabic word is *bint*. The words for pig (*hazir* in Hebrew, *hanzir* in Arabic) and nose (*af* in Hebrew, *anf* in Arabic) are two more examples of the similarities between Hebrew and Arabic. Some have attempted to show a connection between the term *El* used in the Bible and the Arabic word *Allah*. Linguistically, both Hebrew and Arabic are Semitic languages.

Another important aspect of Arab culture was love for the Arabic language. Arab culture was primarily an oral culture. Correctly spoken Arabic was treasured by people of the land, and the purest form of Arabic could be heard among the nomadic groups that moved from place to place. Visitors coming from different parts of the world had not impacted their language. Storytelling and poetry were deeply valued in pre-Islamic Arabia. Poets were highly respected because they spoke with eloquence and because they had connections with the spiritual world. Poetry was not viewed simply as human creativity. Instead, poems ultimately came from the inspiration of spiritual beings called *jinn*, who could be good or evil and who worked their word magic through the mouth of the poet. The term "genie" that later became associated with Aladdin's lamp and even television shows like *I Dream of Genie* was a derivative of the term *jinn*. Those who could speak well were respected for their great love of the Arabic language. Because pre-Islamic Arabs were part of a primarily oral culture, the written form of the language was refined to ensure that the pronunciations would be accurately produced when read aloud.

Pre-Islamic Religious Life

One of the most popular places for the pilgrims was an area in Mecca called the Ka'ba. The word Ka'ba means "cube" and describes a large cube covered with a black cloth. In one portion of the cube a black stone is visible. According to Islamic tradition, Adam established the Ka'ba at the command of God through the angel Gabriel. Later the Ka'ba was reestablished by Abraham and his son Ishmael. In the Jewish and Christian traditions Abraham, as an act of faith, takes Isaac to a mountain area and is prepared to offer him as a sacrifice to

God. God spares Isaac and provides a ram for the burnt offering. In the Islamic tradition, Abraham takes Ishmael to the mountain area, God spares Ishmael, and the two of them journey down to the area now known as Mecca and build an altar that is now known as the Ka'ba. The mountain area where the offering was to be made is believed to be Jerusalem, according to Islamic tradition, and the Dome of the Rock [Mosque] is believed by some to be the site of the actual rock used by Abraham. The rock can be viewed beneath this important mosque. The sacred black stone in the Ka'ba was given by Gabriel to Adam, according to some Islamic traditions, and the stone was restored by Abraham after being absent from the Ka'ba. Today, the Ka'ba represents the holiest Muslim site on earth. When Muslims pray each day, they face in the direction of Mecca and the sacred site of the Ka'ba. Just as Jews respected the Jerusalem temple, Muslims respect the Ka'ba. Millions of Muslims go on a spiritual pilgrimage to the city of Mecca each year and circle the black cube located in the Ka'ba. Although the Ka'ba was intended to honor the one and only God of the universe, by the time of Muhammad's birth the Ka'ba had representations of many deities, the Ka'ba contained symbols and images representing several deities and pilgrims came from afar to honor one or more of these deities. The city of Mecca became dependent on the income generated by the religious pilgrims who journeyed to the Ka'ba each year.

The term *Allah* is the Arabic term for God used by Muslims and Arabic-speaking Christians. According to pre-Islamic religious tradition, Allah was viewed as the supreme god who created the universe. Allah had three daughters who were honored by different tribes. The Qur'an describes this period in Arabia as one of ignorance and mentions the three commonly worshipped gods in pre-Islamic Arabia: *al-Lat*, *al-Uzza*, and *Menat*. Al-Lat was the moon goddess, and some evidence points to the crescent moon as her symbol. Al-Lat was likely revered by a tribe dwelling south of the city of Mecca. Al-Uzza was the goddess of the morning star and was worshipped by the Quraysh tribe, the tribe of Muhammad. Some suggest that human sacrifice was associated with the worship of al-Uzza. Menat was the goddess of fate and time. The worship of Menat included the veneration of a black stone, but according to Arab tradition this was not the same black stone found today in the Ka'ba.

In addition to the polytheistic Arabs, others lived in pre-Islamic Arabia. Both Jewish tribes and groups of Christians could be found in parts of Arabia. Many in Arabia would have had an opportunity to understand at least some of the traditions of the Jews and Christians who lived there. Traditions related to both groups were later included in the Qur'an and in some of the popular stories not found in the Qur'an. The Jewish tribes were located primarily in the south part of Arabia and in Medina.

The Christian communities were likely from the Monophysite, Nestorian, and Mandaean traditions. The Monophysites, who emerged from Ethiopia, believed that Jesus had only a divine nature. The Nestorians believed Jesus had two natures, a divine nature and a human nature, but exhibited only one nature at a time. The Mandaeans (called *Sabians* in the Qur'an) were a gnostic group that venerated John the Baptist, used baptism as a means of purification, used Babylonian astrology, and possibly were related to the Essenes of the Qumran community. The Mandaeans believed Adam was the first Mandaean who was taught by God and given the responsibility to teach those who would come after him. The church at Rome considered these groups heretical. Those who worshipped one God were called *hanifs*, which was the Qur'anic term for a monotheist.

One other monotheistic religious group found in the eastern part of Arabia was the Zoroastrians (called *majus* in the Qur'an). This Persian religion focused on the cosmic battle between good and evil. Zoroastrians believed in the resurrection of the dead, astrology, and the existence of the soul. Today they are identified as the Parsees.

Summary

Pre-Islamic Arabia was in a period of transition and even turmoil during the latter part of the sixth century Into this rugged, tumultuous environment Muhammad was born. He would eventually be seen as one who could bring peace amid the conflict that seemed to ravage the land. In the next chapter, we will see how Islam condemns many of the practices and beliefs of pre-Islamic Arabia. We will also see how some of the values and traditions of pre-Islamic Arabia were adopted and adapted into the community established by Muhammad.[1]

---

[1] For a history of the Arab people, see Albert Hourani, *A History of the Arab Peoples* (London: Faber and Faber Limited, 1991) and Bernard Lewis, *The Arabs in History*, 4th ed. (London: Hutchinson University Library, 1966).

Chapter 2

A PICTURE OF
THE PROPHET MUHAMMAD

Pre-prophetic Years

Muhammad Ibn' Abdallah was born in 570 in the city of Mecca. His name reflects that he was the son of Abdallah. Muhammad faced more than his share of grief during his childhood years. According to Islamic sources, Muhammad's father became ill while visiting his wife's relatives in Medina, died, and was buried in Medina several weeks before Muhammad was born. From the age of eight days until he was either five or six, Muhammad was raised by a Bedouin wet nurse. Arabs felt strongly that a child should be nursed for at least two years to grow strong while learning the pure form of Arabic spoken by the Bedouin. The wet-nursing was common in pre-Islamic Arabia and briefly mentioned in the Qur'an. The practice was common in pre-Islamic Arabia for several reasons: first, parents in wealthy tribes commonly allowed someone else to nurse the child so that the birth mother could have more children sooner; second, some considered wet nursing to be good for the health of the children, especially those born in urban areas; and third, some mothers could not provide adequate milk for their children and needed help from others. Many Bedouin women depended on the practice of wet nursing as a source of income and even sought out potential children for whom they could care. Because Muhammad was fatherless, few wet nurses were attracted to him, as they expected the father to compensate them for their efforts. Muhammad stayed with his wet nurse much longer than usual.

After returning to live with his mother, Muhammad went on his first visit to Medina. On the way back from Medina, Muhammad's mother became ill and died. His paternal grandfather, 'Abd al-Muttalib, took responsibility for the young boy for the next two years of his life. His grandfather died when Muhammad was eight, and an uncle on his mother's side named Abu Talib cared for him until he became an adult. Abu Talib was the leader of the Banu Hashim clan to which Muhammad belonged. Abu Talib later used his influence to protect Muhammad from his Meccan opponents when he began his ministry. During his days with Abu Talib, Muhammad learned how to tend sheep in the tradition of David and Moses. At the age of fifteen, he joined others who pledged to address the unmet needs of the oppressed. At the same age, he was with his uncle when he, Abu Talib, fought in the Fijar (Immoral) War between two of the clans in Muhammad's tribe. Traditions vary as to whether Muhammad actually fought in the war or collected used arrows after the completion of a battle. The war lasted four years and gave Muhammad his first taste of military life. He received recognition for his behavior during the war and was given the name *al-Amin* ("the trustworthy" or "the loyal").

Several Islamic sources include stories concerning Muhammad's birth and early life that some Muslims consider historical and others consider legends. One story suggests that a great light emerged from Muhammad's mother so she could view castles in the Bostra region of Syria.[1] In another tradition, she hears a voice saying her child will be the Lord of his people and that God will protect him from his enemies. Another story emerged from Muhammad's early years with the Bedouin wet nurse. Reportedly, two men dressed in white approached the child, bringing with them a golden bowl filled with snow. They took Muhammad's heart from his body, removed a black clot, cleansed his heart and chest with the snow, and then replaced his purified heart. The reminder of this encounter was said to be a permanent mark on Muhammad's back.

Another of these stories places Muhammad and Abu Talib's family on a journey to Syria when Muhammad was twelve years old. During this journey, they came near the castles seen by his mother before he was born, and there the caravan met a hermit monk named Bahira. Bahira seldom spoke to travelers, but he noticed a cloud that seemed to follow the caravan. He also noted that the tree branches seemed to lower to protect the group from the heat of the day. Uncharacteristically, this hermit invited the whole group for a meal. Muhammad stayed behind to tend the animals. Bahira asked if all had come to join him in the meal, and his guests told him about the one left behind to tend the animals. When he gazed at Muhammad, Bahira knew that Muhammad had been chosen to be a prophet of Allah for the Arab people and would speak the words of Allah to them in the Arabic language. Some traditions suggest that Bahira confirmed Muhammad's identity by looking at the scar on Muhammad's back.[2] These

---

[1] Frederick Mathewson Denny, *An Introduction to Islam*, 3rd ed. (Upper Saddle River NJ: Pearson Education, Inc., 2006) 49.

[2] Ibid., 49–50.

are just a few of the Islamic stories associated with the early life of Muhammad.

As an adult, Muhammad had a reputation for being a reliable and hard worker. He began working for Khadijah, a wealthy widow who made her fortune through caravan trading. Many men hoped to marry this widow, but Muhammad proved to be the one she was prepared to marry. According to Islamic tradition, Muhammad married Khadijah when he was twenty-five years old and she was forty. His family helped provide the twenty young camels needed for the bride price, and Khadijah proved to be his greatest supporter and companion. They had four daughters and two sons together. The first son died at the age of two and the second son died in infancy, but the daughters matured to adulthood. Two of them married men who played significant roles in early Islam. With the resources available to him, Muhammad became a successful businessman in Mecca. During these years, Muhammad also became increasingly appalled at the treatment of orphans, widows, the poor and the practice of infanticide (described in chapter 1).

According to Islamic tradition, at the age of thirty-five, he took part in the renovation of the Ka'ba, which had been damaged by floodwaters. A controversy developed over which group would have the honor of replacing the black stone in the Ka'ba after the repairs were completed. Muhammad reportedly served as a peacemaker by suggesting that a representative from each group hold one portion of a robe that contained the black stone. This reconciliatory act settled the dispute over which group had the right to replace the stone in the Ka'ba. In that same year, Muhammad's youngest daughter, Fatimah, was born.

The worship of Allah displayed by Abraham and the teachings that followed had been swallowed up by images representing one or more of the 360 deities. Pilgrims came from all over the region to honor one or more of the deities in the Ka'ba. Although Muhammad's clan was not wealthy, other clans of his tribe were influential and powerful. These clans acquired significant income from the travelers as they spent money and traded goods. The Ka'ba was an important religious site, but it was also an important economic resource for many people in Mecca. During this time, Muhammad retreated to some of the cave areas outside the city to meditate upon Allah. Some suggest that Muhammad was exposed to the basic teachings of Judaism and Christianity on some of his business trips. Whether or not this was true, he certainly became interested in the worship of the one true God. Both Judaism and Christianity identify themselves as monotheistic religions that trace back to Abraham. During one of Muhammad's cave retreats, his life changed forever as the businessman transformed into a prophet.

Muhammad Becomes a Prophet

In 610 Muhammad went into the caves outside of Mecca where he frequently spent time in meditation. On this occasion, the angel Gabriel approached him and spoke one word: "*Iqraa.*" Traditionally this word is interpreted as "recite," although some suggest that it should be translated "read." Those who believe Allah gave Muhammad, who was illiterate, the ability to read, advocate the latter interpretation. The angel gave him the first revelation of the Qur'an, telling him to recite in the name of Allah who created human beings. Gabriel provided the revelation necessary for human beings to live at peace with God and with each other. The first revelation given to Muhammad is found in chapter 96 of the Qur'an: "Proclaim! [or Read!] In the name of the Lord and Cherisher, who created man, out of a (mere) clot of congealed blood. Proclaim! And thy Lord is Most Bountiful. He Who taught (the use of) the Pen, taught man that which he knew not."[3] Over the next twenty-two years (twenty-three years using the Muslim calendar), Muhammad received revelations from Allah, and the collection of these revelations is known as the Qur'an.

As one might expect, Muhammad was shaken by the initial encounter with Gabriel. He fled from the cave and sought comfort from his wife, Khadijah. She assured him that he should not fear what had taken place because he had chosen a righteous life. Muhammad eventually recognized that Allah had indeed spoken to him through the angel Gabriel and had chosen him as a prophet. His wife Khadijah became the first person to accept Muhammad as a prophet and the first person to embrace Islam. Muhammad learned that his task was to reestablish the worship of the one true God that had been taught to all the prophets of God through the years. Historically he was starting a new religion, but Muslims believe he renewed the religion previously revealed to people like Abraham and Moses. In the midst of Arab polytheism, Muhammad was to call the people back to the worship of the one and only creator of the universe who provided laws that would enable people to live in peace with Allah and humanity.

Six months after his experience in the cave, Muhammad began preaching this message to his family and close friends.

---

[3] *The Holy Qur'an*, trans. A. Yusuf Ali (Brentwood MD: Amana Corporation, 1983).

He waited three years to begin his public ministry in Mecca. Although some received his message in Mecca, he primarily encountered coolness and even hostility.

The early followers of Islam were primarily family members and close friends of Muhammad. Ali, the husband of Muhammad's daughter Fatimah, and Abu Bakr were the first two men who embraced Islam. In the initial three years of Muhammad's ministry, as many as forty people became Muslims. He began to recite the revelations of the Qur'an that called for people to turn away from idols and the worship of false gods because only one God—Allah—exists. The message also proclaimed that a day is coming when Allah will judge all persons according to their obedience to the commands of Allah.

Because many in the city of Mecca were polytheists and because they depended on the money brought in by religious pilgrimages to the Ka'ba, they were often hostile to Muhammad's message and his attempt to convert Arabia to monotheism. The message of Muhammad struck at the heart of their religious traditions and economic livelihood. Citizens of Mecca not only disagreed with Muhammad, but they also sought to stop him from creating havoc in the city. Members of his own tribe attempted to stop Muhammad by bribing him, threatening him, boycotting businesses owned by those who professed Islam, and torturing those who identified themselves as Muslims. Muhammad's uncle Abu Talib squelched the attempts to harm his nephew. The powerful position of Abu Talib as the leader of the Hashim clan allowed Muhammad to continue his ministry under his uncle's protection. Persecution increased until many of the Muslims had to flee to Abyssinia (Ethiopia) for their own safety in 615. In spite of these circumstances, Muhammad continued to proclaim the message of monotheism to the people of Mecca. He could not compromise his responsibility to speak the words he had received from Allah. The Meccans feared the impact of Muhammad's ministry for three reasons: first, they feared that his preaching would bring the wrath of the other deities upon the city of Mecca; second, they feared his preaching of monotheism could have a negative impact on their economy; and third, they were offended and even fearful of the powerful condemnation of the polytheism that they considered to be part of their cultural heritage.

Two significant deaths in 619 made it one of the most difficult years of Muhammad's life. He lost both his beloved wife Khadijah, who had supported him from the beginning of his ministry, and his uncle Abu Talib, who had protected him from the death threats of his opposition in Mecca. Without the support of his wife and the protection of his uncle, Muhammad's ministry entered into a critical period. Two other events related to his uncle's death made matters worse. The new clan leader, who considered Muhammad to be a renegade and dangerous to the unity of the tribe, asked Muhammad if his uncle, Abu Talib, was now in heaven. Muhammad was forced to reply that he was not in heaven because he had never accepted Islam.[4] This was seen as an assault on the pride of the Banu Hashim clan and the Quraysh tribe.

Muhammad had to leave Mecca and seek exile in a city to the southeast. The citizens of this city refused to receive Muhammad as a true prophet of God, and soon he had to

---

[4] W. Montgomery Watt, *Muhammad: Prophet and Statesman* (New York: Oxford University Press, 1961) 80.

return to Mecca. In 620 his fortune began to change when twelve men of Medina invited him to make peace between the feuding tribes and clans in that city. This would prove to be a crucial event in Muhammad's prophetic career. In the same year, he married a fifty-year-old widow who had been in exile in Abyssinia and also married A'ishah, the young daughter of his companion Abu Bakr. Over the next several years, many Muslims were killed in battle and left behind widows. Muhammad married eight more women between 620–629. By the end of his life, he had married either nine or thirteen women.[5] Two of these wives were from Jewish tribes, and one was a Christian slave sent to him by the governor of Egypt. Many of the wives were widows of fallen soldiers. Others he married for political reasons. Toward the end of his ministry, Muhammad received a revelation that limited the number of wives for Muslim men to four.

During the year 621 (B.H. 1), Muhammad had a powerful mystical experience that played an important role in shaping Islam. Chapter 17, verse 1 of the Qur'an mentions that one night Muhammad was at the Ka'ba in Mecca when in a vision he was swept away to the furthest mosque or holy place of prayer (located in Jerusalem): "Glory to [God] who did take His Servant for a Journey by night from the Sacred Mosque to the Farthest Mosque, whose precincts we did bless, in order that We might show him some of Our Signs; for He is the One who heareth and seeth (all things)."[6] He was taken to a sacred place that, according to Islamic tradition, Abraham established. This sacred place was on the site where Solomon's Temple

---

[5] Ibn Ishaq, *Sirat Rasul Allah (The Life of Muhammad)*, trans. A. Guillaume (New York: Oxford University Press, 1955) 792.

[6] Surah 17:1.

once stood. Today the Dome of the Rock rests on a portion of land that held Solomon's Temple. Tradition indicates that the rock underneath the Dome of the Rock Mosque was the one on which Abraham was prepared to present his son Ishmael as an offering to God. At this holy site in Jerusalem, God confirmed that Muhammad was indeed a prophet in the tradition of Abraham and Moses. Although the details are not found in the Qur'an, there are many Muslim traditions related to Muhammad's journey. In this vision, he journeyed to the seventh level of heaven. As he passed from level to level, the prophets of old such as Moses and Jesus greeted him and confirmed his calling as a prophet chosen by God. In the seventh level of heaven, he met Abraham and came into the presence of Allah. He received a command to pray fifty times each day, yet due to the weakness of the people the number was reduced to five times per day. God confirmed Muhammad as a prophet in the long line of prophets and gave instructions for the community that would become one of the pillars of Islam. The mosque built on the site of Muhammad's journey is now considered to be one of the holiest mosques in the world. The Muslim community began praying five times a day as a result of Muhammad's mystical journey. Since Muhammad had journeyed to Jerusalem, the Muslims began praying daily in the direction of Jerusalem. Later, all Muslim prayers would be directed to the city of Mecca.

Other traditions not found in the Qur'an are associated with this event in Muhammad's life. Some suggest that Muhammad led all the prophets who had come before him in prayer. In another tradition, Muhammad is presented with three golden vessels—one filled with milk, one with water, and one with wine. Muhammad is asked to choose between the vessels. He chooses the milk and drinks it. This represents Muhammad choosing good over evil.[7] Muslims believe children naturally desire to choose the good until the world corrupts them. Other stories include Muhammad seeing the territory that would eventually receive Islam, a vision of persons who refused to submit to God in the torture of hell, and a vision of camel herds in Mecca. All the events of this mystical experience supposedly took place in one night. Muslims today are not in agreement as to whether Muhammad actually traveled to heaven physically or if this was a spiritual vision. In either case, the event is seen as a confirmation of the role of Muhammad as a true prophet of God.[8]

This experience produced at least two results. Muhammad was more certain than ever of his calling to be a prophet of God, as were those who accepted the details of his journey, but those who opposed him increased their efforts to stop him. In 622 a plot developed to assassinate Muhammad, but the angel Gabriel warned him of this plot and he fled the city safely. He and the other Muslims migrated to Medina. Most around him did not recognize the significance of this journey. The day the Muslims left Mecca to journey to Medina was the first step in their transformation from a small group of misunderstood monotheists into a religious and political force in Arabia. The Muslim calendar begins with the day when Muhammad and his group embarked on their journey to Medina.[9] Medina would

---

[7] Ishaq, *Muhammad*, 182.

[8] For a detailed description of Muhammad's life in Mecca see W. Montgomery Watt's *Muhammad at Mecca* (New York: Oxford University Press, 1953).

[9] Muslims use a lunar calendar in which every month has 29 or 30 days and a year has 354 days, 8 hours, and 40 minutes, whereas the solar

provide an environment for Islam to achieve the status of a free standing global religion.

A New Day Dawns in Medina

For the first time the Muslim community could live in relative peace and security. Muhammad had converted influential members of Medina in 620, and they had converted others to Islam. When Muhammad arrived in Medina in 622, the recent converts welcomed him. Instead of having to endure persecution and protect himself from plots against his life, Muhammad could now freely establish the Muslim community in a city that would receive him. This community would observe the laws given to him. The direction of prayer changed from Jerusalem to Mecca during Muhammad's time in Medina. Some scholars have suggested that this change resulted from the Christians and Jews rejecting Muhammad as a prophet of God, but most Muslims believe the change took place after the Ka'ba had been purified from all forms of polytheistic worship. Muhammad could not pray in the direction of the Ka'ba until all the idols had been destroyed.

Muhammad would become a statesman and, when necessary, a military leader in Medina. He would eventually make a treaty with the non-Muslims in Medina so peace could be established. Many of the warring tribes found in Islam the motivation to live and work together as one community. Loyalty reserved for one's tribe now became loyalty to the new tribe, the Muslim community. Unfortunately the peace found in Medina was short lived as Muhammad's enemies in Mecca

---

calendar has 365.25 days. See Cyril Glassé, *The Concise Encyclopedia of Islam* (New York: HarperCollins Publishers, 1989) 82.

sought to destroy him and the message that threatened their way of life.

In 624, a few hundred Muslims sought to attack a Meccan caravan near Badr, and they encountered a much larger Meccan army that was protecting the caravan. Islamic tradition suggests that Muhammad learned the caravan contained materials intended for an attack on the Muslim community in Medina. Although outnumbered three to one, Muhammad led his troops into battle and defeated the larger army. The victory won Muhammad great respect because Arabs always treasured individuals who displayed valor in battle. The defeat was a blow to the reputation of the Meccans.

The following year, the Meccans sought revenge. Desiring to establish a safe trade route near Medina, they planned an attack on Muhammad and the Muslim community. A large army attacked Muhammad and his troops just outside the city. The Muslim army succeeded for a time, but Muhammad was wounded and his uncle killed. The Meccan army seemed to be on the verge of destroying the Muslim army, and the city of Medina lay before them undefended. Then the Meccan army surprisingly left the battlefield and returned to Mecca, possibly because they believed Muhammad was dead. The Meccan army did not enter Medina to complete the seemingly inevitable victory. Although the Muslims appeared to be nearly defeated, they viewed the Meccans' retreat as a sign of Allah's protection. Though they clearly did not win the battle, the survival of Muhammad and the city of Medina lifted the spirits of the Muslim community.

Two years later, the Meccans returned to Medina with a massive army of 10,000, intending to end the feud once and for all. The Muslim army dug a trench that was used for the defense of the city, and the combat that followed became known as the Battle of the Trench. The Meccan army made one attempt after another to cross the trench. Their inability to cross it left them unable to take the city of Medina. Successfully defending the city against such a large army further boosted the morale of the Muslim community in Mecca, and many non-Muslims continued to convert to Islam.

Three battles were fought with the Meccans over a period of four years. By military standards, the Muslims clearly won the first battle and lost the second battle. The third battle was a draw. Yet the Muslim community drew strength from all three battles because they proved that Allah was indeed protecting them and their prophet, Muhammad. The young boy from a meager background was now a highly respected warrior, statesman, and prophet. Some sources point to the involvement of a Jewish tribe who threw their support behind the Meccan army. By 628, Muhammad had established a secure base in Medina for the Muslim community. They had shown that they could weather the Meccan storm. The next step was to secure the city of Mecca so that the Muslims could worship freely at the Ka'ba and destroy all the images used by polytheistic pilgrims.

Going Home Again

In 628, Muhammad brought 1,000 Muslims on a pilgrimage to the Ka'ba in Mecca. Men from the city came out to meet Muhammad, and a treaty was formed between Mecca and Medina. The treaty established peace between the two cities and made provision for Muhammad and the other Muslims to make an annual pilgrimage to Mecca beginning the following year. The group from Medina returned home in peace knowing that they were free to return the next year to worship at the Ka'ba in peace. The treaty was supposed to last ten years and allowed Muslims from Medina to come unarmed into Mecca to fulfill their religious quest. The treaty also made it easier for Islam to be proclaimed and for people to join the movement. That same year, Muhammad took control of a Jewish fortress. In return for half of their produce, the residents were able to stay in the land and assured protection by Muhammad and his troops. The practice of allowing a conquered people to remain in exchange for an annual due became normative as Islam spread beyond Arabia, but this practice only applied to those who were monotheists.

In 629, 2,000 unarmed Muslims from Medina made their way to the holy city of Mecca to worship at the Ka'ba. The Meccans assured peace by vacating the city to avoid conflict between the two groups. The pilgrimage to Mecca lasted for several days and included seven circuits around the black stone in the outer area of the Ka'ba, seven trips between two hills, the sacrifice of a camel, and the shaving of Muhammad's head. Muhammad wanted to enter the Ka'ba itself, but the locals refused to give him the key and told him the contract did not grant him that right. At the end of 629, some Meccan troops broke the treaty by attacking an ally of Medina.

Early in 630, Muhammad gathered 10,000 men to travel to Mecca to avenge the breaking of the treaty. The leader of the Meccan forces—Muhammad's father-in-law—came out to meet Muhammad. When he saw the size of the army from Medina, he basically surrendered the city to Muhammad. Mecca, and particularly the Ka'ba, could now be liberated from the idolatry that had been protected and promoted by the city leaders. Muhammad went to the Ka'ba, circled it seven times, and then purified the holy site by destroying all the idols that had been placed there. The holy site that was once dedicated to the one and only God of the universe was now rededicated to Allah. Muhammad purged idolatry from the Ka'ba and, eventually, Arabia. After purifying the Ka'ba, he went to the Temple of al-Uzza, the goddess of his own tribe, and destroyed the building and the idol representing the goddess. From there he fought a large army protecting the Temple of al-Lat. After a difficult battle, the Muslims destroyed the temple in an event that came to represent the abolishment of polytheism in Arabia.

Muhammad attempted to convert citizens from the Persian and Byzantine empires, both of which held lands in or near Arabia. He sent letters to leaders of the areas, but they did not respond to his invitation to accept Islam. Eventually, circumstances led to battles with Byzantine forces in northern Arabia and in Syria. The Byzantine Empire was a Christian empire with its headquarters in Constantinople or what is today known as Istanbul in Turkey. Some converted to Islam, and those who were Jews and Christians could continue to practice their religion if they agreed to pay an annual fee. Arab polytheists were given three days to convert or to die by the sword. The goal was to establish monotheism throughout Arabia with Jews and Christians remaining under the Islamic protectorate. Most of the residents in Mecca converted to Islam, and by the end of 630 the majority of Arabia was Muslim. Within the next two years, Arabia and some surrounding areas came under the control of the Muslim community.

During the pilgrimage season of 632, Muhammad preached his final sermon as he grew increasingly ill. Some

Islamic sources suggest that Muhammad had the choice of becoming wealthy and remaining alive until the Day of Judgment or entering into the paradise of heaven. These sources state that Muhammad chose to enter paradise. In June of that year, Muhammad breathed his last in the arms of his wife A'ishah.[10] He had accomplished his task of uniting Arabia under the name of Allah, which, according to the Qur'an (14:35–41), was the prayer of Abraham.[11]

The man who began life in meager circumstances emerged as a statesman, military leader, and prophet of Allah. Arabia had become united under the flag of Islam. Byzantine armies in Syria had been defeated, and Islam expanded beyond Arabia. Medina proved to be the turning point in Muhammad's mission. In the city of Mecca, Muhammad had been persecuted and rejected by many, but in Medina the Muslims grew into a powerful force. Muhammad transformed from a persecuted prophet warning of the Day of Judgment into the apostle of Allah who established the Muslim community dedicated to obeying Allah's commands. Islam transformed from a small Meccan movement into a powerful force that would forever change the political and religious landscape of Arabia. It became a world religion that would move far beyond the borders of Arabia. The prophet of Allah had established Islam and wiped out the polytheistic practices in all of Arabia.

The revelations Muhammad had received would be gathered together as the Qur'an. The actions and other sayings

---

[10] Ibn Ishaq, *Muhammad*, 678.

[11] For a more in-depth description of Muhammad's life in Medina, see W. Montgomery Watt's *Muhammad at Medina* (New York: Oxford University Press, 1956).

of the prophet, referred to as the Sunnah, would be collected by many different sources and eventually put in writing as the Hadith. In the years following Muhammad's death various scholars attempted to preserve the sayings of Muhammad and other important Muslims. These were used to address issues not clearly addressed in the Qur'an. Today, several different Hadith collections are used including Sahih Bukhari, Sahih Muslim, Sunan Abu-Dawvd, and Malik's Muwatta. Many Muslim scholars challenge the historicity of much of the Hadith material. The Qur'an and the traditions of the prophet established the foundation of Islamic law. The next chapter focuses on the teachings of the Qur'an that shaped Islamic theology and practice.

Chapter 3

A PICTURE OF
THE QUR'AN

This chapter explores some of the basic teachings found in the Qur'an. When appropriate, I have also included non-Qur'anic sources as a sample of commonly accepted Islamic teachings not found in the Qur'an.

Introductory Matters

The term *qur'an* means recitation. As stated earlier, the first word spoken by the angel Gabriel to Muhammad was "recite." These revelations came to Muhammad from 610 until his death in 632. As mentioned in chapter 1, pre-Islamic Arabians treasured the pure form of Arabic as the language of heaven, and those who could orate poems or stories were highly regarded. The Qur'an was revealed in Arabic, and, according to Muslim tradition, it must continue to be recited in Arabic.[1] As Islam spread into non-Arabic-speaking lands, the primacy of Arabic was maintained. Even today, many Muslims feel that other translations of the Qur'an serve as helpful commentaries, but they maintain the need for the Qur'an to be recited in Arabic.

---

[1] Cyril Glassé, *The Concise Encyclopedia of Islam* (New York: HarperCollins Publishers, 1991, 2nd ed.) 47, 231.

The Qur'an contains 114 surahs or chapters that are basically organized from the longest revelation to the shortest, with the exception of the first chapter, which is titled "The Opening." No clear reason is given for the organization of the chapters of the Qur'an. Chapters are named for a *person* (examples include Abraham [14]; Mary [19]; Jonah [10]; Joseph, [12]), an *animal* (examples include the cow [2]; the bee [16]; the ant [27]; the spider [29]), a *theme* (examples include women [4]; the pilgrimage [22]; divorce [65]; resurrection [75]), and many other categories. Because they are ordered from longest to shortest chapters, the revelations may have occurred at any time in Muhammad's life. One of the first revelations of the Qur'an may appear before or after one of the latest revelations of the Qur'an. The reader usually requires some assistance to determine whether a given chapter was revealed during Muhammad's ministry in Mecca or in Medina. Islamic scholars place each chapter in one of four categories: Early Meccan, Middle Meccan, Late Meccan, and Medinan. The Early Meccan revelations are usually much shorter than the later revelations. The Middle Meccan revelations and Late Meccan revelations are longer and focus heavily on the characters also found in the Bible. The Medinan revelations deal with legal and social matters. Muslims view the Qur'an as Allah's gift to the world to tell them how to live in peace with him and with each other.[2] According to Islam, the Qur'an represents the most reliable revelation available to humankind today.

---

[2] This chapter includes many Qur'anic references. Each reference in the footnotes begins with the word "Surah," which means chapter, followed by the chapter number in the Qur'an, a colon, and then the verse or verses that relate to the point in the text.

Qur'anic View of Allah and Allah's Creation

The Qur'an affirms Allah as the one and only God who exists. From an environment in which hundreds of gods could be worshipped emerged a religion that established, or reestablished, absolute monotheism. Any attempt to compare anyone or anything to Allah is an affront to the heart of Islam. Traditional Islam discourages images of people, including Muhammad, for fear that one might compare their authority or popularity with Allah. Many Muslims considered pictures of Saddam Hussein that were plastered throughout Baghdad unhealthy and bordering on idolatry. For Muslims, only one God exists—the one to whom they refer as Allah.

One must remember that Arab Christians also use the term *Allah* to refer to God. Although the Qur'an does not describe Allah in detail, Islam uses as many as ninety-nine names to refer to Allah. Many Muslims use prayer beads to recite the ninety-nine beautiful names of God. One important term the Qur'an uses is "Lord." Allah is described as the creator of the universe and its Lord. Many people from the United States and Europe believe the Qur'an portrays Allah as vengeful and brutal. Although many of the terms refer to the power of God, all but one chapter of the Qur'an begin with the words "In the name of Allah, the Merciful, the Compassionate." This phrase is called the *Bismillah*. Many Muslims suggest that this phrase captures the heart of Islam in that every Muslim is to do all things in the name of Allah. The fact that God stands alone is also a call for all humanity to be obedient to the instructions of Allah on how to live. No human can fully understand Allah because Allah is greater than human comprehension, yet by following the guidance of the Qur'an individuals can be at peace with Allah.[3] The Muslim community is to submit to the unity of God and unite with each other through submission to Allah.

The Qur'an portrays Allah as the protector and sustainer of all creation.[4] Allah's bounties are open to all living things. While described as merciful and compassionate, one must also understand that Allah chooses to display mercy and compassion whenever and with whomever Allah chooses. In other words, mercy and compassion should not be expected in all circumstances, but when they are given they should be deeply appreciated. God is described as all powerful, all knowing, and everlasting.[5] The Qur'an also states that Allah has no sons; therefore, Jesus and the other prophets were created by Allah.[6] The primary focus of the Qur'an is not on the character of God, but rather on the will of God for all creation. According to Islam, one does not use the Qur'an to understand God because God is beyond our ability to understand.

Allah Creates Spiritual Beings

Angels are some of the special spiritual beings created by Allah. Gabriel and Michael are the only two named angels in the Qur'an, but passages related to angels unwrap the Qur'anic view of human beings.[7] Angels were created to serve as Allah's messengers and helpers. The Qur'an teaches that angels were

---

[3] Surah 40:82.
[4] Surah 3:108.
[5] Surah 51:58; 2:115; 6:59.
[6] Surah 72:3.
[7] Surah 2:97–98.

created from light and are by nature good and loyal to Allah. Other spiritual beings created by Allah were the jinn. Chapter 72 of the Qur'an is titled "Jinn," or "the Spirits." The jinn are described as spiritual beings created from fire that can be either good or evil.[8] The jinn were part of the pre-Islamic worldview and the inspiration for poems in pre-Islamic Arabia (see chapter 1).

A specific creation of Allah was Satan, called *Iblis* (Devil) and *Shaitan* (Satan) in the Qur'an. Some Muslims consider Satan to be a fallen angel, but the Qur'an identifies him as one of the jinn. Some Islamic sources link the two traditions by declaring that the jinn were originally angels who were later cast out of heaven. The Qur'an describes the jinn as being created from a smokeless fire and indicates that a jinn is appointed for each person at birth.[9] The jinn heard the recitation of the Qur'an and were pleased, but often jinn are described as being supportive of Satan's rebellious spirit instead of submitting to the will of Allah. Satan deceives people, drives people to hatred, and promotes vanity. Although Satan has no power over the Muslim, he can tempt them to turn their backs on Allah. When Allah created the first man, Adam, Allah demanded the angels bow down before him to recognize their subservient place. All of the angels complied, but the Qur'an records that Satan refused to bow before Adam.[10]

---

[8] Surah 15:27.
[9] Surah 15:27.
[10] Surah 18:50.

Allah Creates Nature

Allah created all the creatures, the trees, the oceans, and the sky. Nature represents a sign of the power and majesty of Allah. The natural order of nature points to Allah's sense of unity. The heavens and the earth declare praises to Allah.[11] The Qur'an declares that Allah makes the clouds move and sends rain from the skies. Allah acts in creation as Allah pleases. Allah causes daylight and nightfall. Allah created and rules over the creatures found throughout the world. The description of Allah creating the world resembles the accounts given in the book of Genesis in the Bible. Allah created the world in six days simply by saying "Be."[12]

Allah Creates Human Beings

In the Qur'an, Allah creates man from clay, similar to the Genesis account, but the Qur'an also describes humanity as coming from a drop of sperm into a blood clot, which grew into a fetus. Bones and flesh were then added so that Adam came into existence as the first human being.[13] From the beginning, man was destined to die and be raised up on the Day of Judgment. Adam was the name of the first man created by Allah for the purpose of serving Allah as a deputy or representative on the earth.[14] Allah taught Adam the nature of all things and told him to name the animals.[15] Adam was given a wife who would share life with him in the bountiful garden

---

[11] Surah 17:44.
[12] Surah 36:82.
[13] Surah 22:5.
[14] Surah 2:30.
[15] Surah 2:31.

where Allah placed him. Allah created human beings as superior to the angels because they have the ability to choose to follow or to disobey Allah.

Adam and his wife were living in the beautiful garden provided by Allah until Satan led them to follow their temptations. Similar to the account in Genesis 3, the couple was removed from the garden after they disobeyed God, and they were made to work the earth for their livelihood.[16] Although the story resembles the Genesis account, Muslims do not consider the first humans' expulsion as the foundation of original sin.[17] The Qur'an also tells of the two sons of Adam who both offered a sacrifice to Allah, but one of the sacrifices was not acceptable.[18] The one who had his offering rejected killed his brother because he was jealous. This story resembles the story of Cain and Abel in Genesis 4. Allah commanded Adam and his descendants to serve Allah throughout their life, although like Adam they must beware of the basic human weakness to give in to one's lower instincts.

Ultimately, every human being must give an account of his or her faithfulness to Allah's commands. The prayer of the Muslim from the Qur'an is for the strength to follow the straight path of obedience and not to swerve to the left or to the right.

---

[16] Surah 20:120–23.

[17] Original sin was a doctrine traced to Augustine of Hippo who suggested that all human beings are born sinners due to Adam's failure to resist temptation in Genesis 3.

[18] Surah 5:30–34.

Qur'anic View of Humanity

The Qur'an declares that Allah created human beings from a clot of blood, from clay, and from water.[19] Such simple sources remind humans that they do not compare to Allah, but that they are merely one of Allah's many creations. The Qur'an also describes humans as unique among all of Allah's creation in that they possess knowledge and free will, but the Qur'an also provides fertile ground for a doctrine that God ordains all human activity. According to the Qur'an, Allah breathed his breath into Adam and the man became a living soul, *naf*.[20] The price of having a free will is that Allah also demands accountability.[21] The duty of every human being is to submit to the will of God their life as an individual and their life in the community of faith. Fear of God is essential in order for human beings to know their place before the creator of all.[22] The focus of the Qur'an is instructing humanity on how to live in harmony with Allah and with each other.

Human beings are to be willing to struggle with their own obedience to Allah and to defend the cause of Allah when necessary. Striving for goodness and serving God are the goals of every human being.[23] The Qur'an recognizes that all human beings struggle to obey Allah because of their propensity for disobedience.[24] Eventually, every Muslim will fail in their attempt to submit to Allah because personal and corporate piety are not easily achieved.

---

[19] Surah 22:5.
[20] Surah 15:29.
[21] Surah 10:47.
[22] Surah 2:2.
[23] Surah 3:110; 51:56.
[24] Surah 4:28.

Allah Speaks to Humanity

Throughout history, Allah has communicated with humanity so that they might know how to live in peace with Allah and with each other. One way Allah speaks to human beings is through angels.[25] Gabriel was the angel who revealed the Qur'an to Muhammad, and Michael is also mentioned in the Qur'an.[26] God also speaks to the human race through prophets.[27] The Qur'an mentions twenty-five different prophets, some of whose names are also found in the Bible. Noah, Abraham, Elijah, Ezekiel, Isaac, Jacob, Job, and Aaron are a few of the prophets mentioned in the Qur'an who are important Old Testament figures. Some of the prophets mentioned in the Qur'an can also be found in the New Testament. Zechariah (father of John the Baptist), John the Baptist, and John are all considered prophets in the Qur'an. Some prophets mentioned in the Qur'an, such as Dhul-Kifl, Hud, and Shuaib, have no parallel reference in the Bible. Through the prophets, Allah continued to call humanity to establish a way of life that would honor him and create a community dedicated to his guiding principles.

The third way Allah communicates with humanity is through revealed Scriptures. Four people in the Qur'an are esteemed as apostles who received a writing from Allah that was for the guidance of humanity. The first to receive a written revelation, according to Islam, was the Apostle Moses, who received the Torah.[28] The Torah refers to the first five books

---

[25] Surah 35:1.
[26] See discussion on page 38.
[27] Surah 4:152.
[28] Surah 11:110.

of the Bible, although some Muslims suggest that the Torah used by Jews and Christians has been altered from its original revelation. The Qur'an tells of Moses being placed in a chest as a baby and hidden in a river to spare his life, leading the Israelites, combating Pharaoh, traveling through the sea in a tunnel, and getting angry when the people built a golden calf. All of these stories resemble accounts found in the Hebrew Bible/Old Testament. The Qur'an refers to signs used to convince Pharaoh to free the Israelites, but only nine signs (ten in the Bible) were used, and the sorcerers of Pharaoh fell down and acknowledged God after Moses' staff consumed theirs.[29]

The second written revelation came to the Apostle David, who received the Psalms.[30] The story of David's defeat of Goliath is told in the Qur'an and in the Hebrew Bible/Old Testament.[31] David is described in the Qur'an as a man of wisdom, sound judgment, and courage. He was commanded by Allah to serve as both a judge and an example so that those around him would follow the straight path of obedience to Allah.[32]

The third revelation came to the Apostle Jesus, who received the Gospel.[33] The Qur'an refers to Jesus in 11 of its 114 chapters. According to the Qur'an, Jesus was born to the virgin Mary, had disciples, taught his disciples compassion and mercy, performed miracles, and was perfectly obedient to the will of Allah. These teachings concerning Jesus in the Qur'an are presented in a way that is similar to the ministry of Jesus

---

[29] Surah 17:101; 7:103–37.
[30] Surah 4:163.
[31] Surah 2:251–52.
[32] Surah 38:20–27.
[33] Surah 5:49, 113.

found in the New Testament. Other Qur'anic teachings concerning Jesus present stories not found in the New Testament, including Jesus being able to speak from the crib and, as a child, making a clay bird that came to life and flew away.[34] The Qur'an states that Jesus and his disciples were Muslims because they submitted to the will of Allah.[35] Jesus made no claims about being God, according to the Qur'an, nor was he the Son of God since Allah has no sons.[36] The Qur'an holds that Jesus was not crucified, but that Allah raised him up before his enemies could cause him harm.[37] He ascended to Allah, and on the Day of Judgment Jesus will acknowledge that he did not teach his disciples the Christian doctrine of trinity.[38]

According to the Qur'an, Jesus predicted the coming of Ahmad, who some Muslims believe is a reference to Muhammad.[39] The prediction of Ahmad coming resembles the New Testament passages when Jesus predicted the coming of the Holy Spirit. The Qur'an suggests that the reason for Muhammad's appearance in Arabia was the unwillingness of the Arab people to accept the prophet Moses or Jesus.[40]

The fourth and final apostle of Islam, according to the Qur'an, was Muhammad.[41] Muhammad received the Qur'an as the fourth scripture given by Allah to the world. Chapter 2 above details the life and ministry of Muhammad. The

---

[34] Surah 19:29–34; 5:113.

[35] Surah 3:52.

[36] Surah 9:30.

[37] Surah 4:157.

[38] Surah 4:171.

[39] Surah 61:6.

[40] Surah 61:5–9.

[41] Surah 33:40.

significance of Muhammad is that he is the last or seal of the
prophets, according to Islam. In the same way a law passed by
the United States Congress replaces any earlier laws, the
Qur'anic revelation is believed to replace all previous
revelations of God.

Allah Guides Humanity

Although chapter 4 addresses the development and
implementation of Islamic law, we must look at five of the
guiding principles given in the Qur'an that are often called the
Five Pillars of Islam. Emerging during Muhammad's life, each
of these pillars is a mandatory part of every Muslim's life.

Shahadah. The first pillar of Islam is the basic confession
of faith "I bear witness that there is no God, but God and
Muhammad is his Apostle or Messenger."[42] The Shahadah or
the confession of faith must be spoken in Arabic. For many
Muslims, the recitation of the confession in Arabic confirms
that the one who speaks it has become or is a Muslim. This
confession is spoken at all significant events in the life of a
Muslim and during the daily prayer or worship.

The Shahadah includes two confessions. First, believers
acknowledge that no other God exists except the God who is
called Allah. Muslims declare their belief in absolute
monotheism in a way similar to how Jews and Christians
declare that only one God exists. Second, Muslims declare
their belief that God chose Muhammad to be a messenger to
the Arab people and ultimately to the world. The first part of
the Shahadah presents the big picture, and the second part

---

[42] Surah 27:60; 33:40. Also see Glassé, *Encyclopedia*, 359–60.

acknowledges the specific role of Muhammad as the messenger or apostle of Islam.

Salat. The second pillar of Islam is the daily ritual prayers or worship.[43] In the early morning, at noon, in the afternoon, at sunset, and in the evening, Muslims are to praise Allah and submit themselves to the will of Allah. The Jewish tradition established prayer three times each day, but the same tradition points to pious persons such as David who modeled prayer five times each day. The times of prayer mark the various transitions of the day and were established following Muhammad's journey described in chapter 2 above. Muslims all over the world offer the same basic prayer in the Arabic language. The direction of the prayers is always toward Mecca. On each Friday at noon, the community gathers for the Community Prayer service, which usually includes a brief sermon or lecture from the Qur'an.

Prayers are offered at funerals and other important events in the life of the Muslim. "Worship" is often a better translation for *salat* because it is a fixed ritual prayer as opposed to an individual person speaking whatever is upon one's heart. The *salat* would be similar to a Christian saying the Apostles Creed or the Lord's Prayer five times each day. Although the Muslim can express personal and corporate concerns to Allah, the salat is designed to be a global worship service in which worshippers remember the Lordship of Allah. Prayers may be performed individually or in a group. If the salat is performed in a group, then one individual should take the leadership role in the prayer. The prayer includes the physical motions of standing, bowing, sitting on one's legs facing forward, and

---

[43] Glassé, *Encyclopedia*, 345–49.

prostrating oneself with the forehead touching the carpet of the mosque or prayer rug.

An important part of preparing for prayer is purification. Before performing the *salat*, one must undergo a ritual washing that includes the washing of one's face, hands and arms to the elbow, head, and feet to the ankles.[44] Purification is important to Muslims at other times as well. One should be ritually pure before handling or reading from the Qur'an. One should remain pure by keeping the dietary restrictions of Islam and by avoiding alcohol. (See chapter 9 for more on Muslim dietary restrictions.) Muslim tradition holds that running water should be used in the purification process for prayer. When running water is not available, one may take water and pour it on from a container to create a similar effect. In the absence of water, a Muslim may use clean sand or dirt for purification.

Zakat. The third pillar of Islam can be translated "almsgiving," though the mandatory zakat actually takes the form of a tax.[45] The word for optional almsgiving to the poor or the needy is *sadaqat*. Zakat was originally designed to aid the widows and orphans of Arabian society. Aside from aiding those in need, the giving of alms reminds Muslim of their dependence on God and is a way to give thanks for their blessings. Today, additional uses for zakat include aiding Muslims in serious debt, travelers in need, those serving Allah in some capacity as missionaries or in the military, and relief projects. Debate currently exists on how the zakat should be used in Muslim countries. See chapter 8 for a discussion of the debate.

---

[44] Surah 5:7.
[45] Glassé, 430–31.

The basic tax rate is 2 1/2 percent of one's wealth with certain properties being taxed at a higher rate. Land is usually taxed at the rate of 10 percent. Dwellings and personal possessions are not subject to the tax. The idea of zakat is to tax things that are beyond what is needed to survive; in this way, the tax does not place the giver into an economic crisis.[46]

Sawm. The fourth pillar of Islam refers to the month-long fast during the month of Ramadan.[47] Each Muslim is expected to fast from the time of day when they can distinguish a white thread from a black thread until the sun sets. The fast includes no eating, drinking, smoking, or marital relations from sunrise to sunset. Far from a somber or sad occasion, the fast is intended to be a joyous event reminding Muslims that all they have is due to the mercy of Allah. The only persons in the community excused from the fast are young children, older adults, travelers, those who are sick, pregnant women, and soldiers on active duty. Those temporarily unable to fast during Ramadan are encouraged to fast during another month.

Many significant events in Islamic history have occurred during the month of Ramadan. Ali, the son-in law and cousin of Muhammad, was born during the month of Ramadan. Other historical happenings during this month include the assassination of Ali, the birth of his son Husayn, and the assassination of the eighth Shi'a Imam al-Rida. Chapter 9 provides additional information on how the fast is observed as part of the Muslim calendar.

Fasting can be done anytime during the year and is encouraged in recognition of important events in the history of Islam. Yet, the only required fasting for all Muslims takes place

---

[46] Ibid.
[47] Ibid., 122, 329–30.

during the month of Ramadan. A cannon may be fired to begin or end the period of fasting during Ramadan.[48]

Hajj. The fifth and final pillar of Islam is the journey to Mecca, or pilgrimage, that every Muslim should take at least once in a lifetime if possible.[49] Muhammad modeled the journey, which is intended to reenact the actions of Abraham and his son Ishmael. The pilgrimage (*hajj*) takes place during the month of Hajj in the Islamic calendar. One begins by circling seven times around the black stone located in a large pillar in the center of the Ka'ba, reenacting Muhammad's purification of the Ka'ba. During the last rotation, the pilgrim attempts to touch or kiss the black stone and offer a personal prayer (not the *salat*) to God. The pilgrim then offers the salat at place called the station of Abraham, which is supposed to bear an imprint of his foot in stone. Following the prayer, the pilgrim drinks from the Zam Zam well discovered by Ishmael, according to Islamic tradition. The pilgrim then travels to two specific hills and walks between them seven times.

The second day of the pilgrimage is the day of standing in which the pilgrim arrives at a location called Arafat. The pilgrim usually spends from noon until night in this location, reflecting on Abraham's decision to sacrifice his son Ishmael.

The third day celebrates the deliverance of Ishmael as God provided a replacement ram. It is also the day of sacrifice

---

[48] I can remember being in a restaurant in Istanbul where people were sitting at tables ready to eat as soon as the cannon was fired to end the day's fast. I can also remember boys in rural Turkey beating a pan with a wooden spoon to wake everyone so they could eat before sunrise and more easily endure the daily fast. Some Muslims believe that volunteering for such a duty is worthy of spiritual merit.

[49] Ibid., 313–16.

as a camel, ox, or ram is offered to commemorate the sparing of Ishmael. This sacrifice is made by the pilgrims and by Muslims all over the world who are not taking part in the actual pilgrimage. A portion of the meat is to be offered to the poor in recognition that God provided the sacrifice. Because Ishmael apparently threw pebbles at an evil apparition, pilgrims also pick up stones that they will cast at a column to represent a rejection of the temptations of Satan.[50] Following these two events, a lock of hair is clipped from each pilgrim. Women may have this done symbolically, and men may have their heads completely shaved.

The remaining days of the pilgrimage are called the days of the drying meat because the sacrifices are left to dry out. Attempts have been made to distribute the unused meat to those in need. The remaining time is used to throw stones at three more pillars, which may take a great deal of time if the number of pilgrims exceeds one million.[51]

The pilgrimage can be taken during any month of the year, but it would be considered a lesser hajj if not taken during the month of Hajj. (See chapter 9 for more information on the hajj.)

Allah Unites Humanity

Although every single Muslim is responsible for submitting to the will of Allah, the Muslim is also accountable to the Muslim community. The first chapter describes the importance of tribal unity in pre-Islamic society and how a sense of loyalty became attached to the larger Muslim community. Just as

---

[50] Frederick Mathewson Denny, *An Introduction to Islam*, 3rd ed. (Upper Saddle River NJ: Pearson Education, Inc., 2006) 134.

[51] Glassé, *Encyclopedia*, 314–16.

Allah is one, the Muslim community should be one. Even though nationalism has created separate Muslim countries around the world, Muslims still feel a certain brotherhood with other Muslims worldwide. Just as an attack upon the tribe would cause a reaction, the Muslim community around the world feels obligated to respond to an unjust attack on a localized Muslim community. This factor complicates foreign relations for most Western countries and the United Nations, as living in a Muslim country provides a strong incentive to observe the five pillars of Islam, dietary restrictions, and other Muslim customs.

Another part of maintaining the unity and existence of the Muslim community is being willing to come to the defense of Allah and the Muslim community when needed. The term *jihad* is an often used, often misunderstood, and often abused term in the twenty-first century. Although most Muslims do not consider jihad to be one of the pillars, some groups consider it the sixth pillar of Islam. The term *jihad* literally means "struggle" and primarily refers to every Muslim's struggle to submit to the will of Allah. Secondarily, jihad refers to an action that defends the cause of Allah.[52] The reformation of an educational system or the creation of a needed social program could be one form of jihad. Jihad can also refer to the taking up of arms in defense against an aggressor. An example of this would be Iraq's invasion of Kuwait. Since Iraq was considered the aggressor when they invaded Kuwait, then anyone who fought to defend Kuwait would be rightfully participating in a jihad. Once allied bombers entered into Iraqi airspace for the first time, Iraqis declared that they were

---

[52] Denny, *Introduction*, 126.

fighting a jihad war (since they were responding to allied aggression). Although the term can be translated "holy war," one must recognize that it has a much broader understanding than simply participating in an armed conflict. Also, jihad can never rightly be used to justify aggression. Jihad, properly understood, refers only to the defense against an aggressor.

Allah Judges Humanity

As mentioned earlier, the Qur'an teaches that Allah will judge individuals based on their deeds. The blasting of the trumpet will announce the Judgment Day of Allah, and the dead will be raised and judged.[53] Only Allah knows the hour of the final judgment.[54] Unbelievers will be raised up to see and hear the reality of hell. Those who rejected the faith will be raised up blind. All forms of false worship will be exposed and their followers at the mercy of Allah.[55] Justice will be served based on one's actions recorded in the Book of Deeds. The Qur'an pictures a weighing of one's deeds on a scale that determines whether the good deeds outweigh the bad ones.[56]

According to the Qur'an, the earth will be pounded to a powder and the heavens rolled up like a scroll.[57] The Qur'an states that Jesus will chastise those who worshipped him or Mary instead of Allah, but Allah may choose to forgive them if Allah so chooses.[58] All differences within the Muslim community will be resolved on the Day of Judgment. No one can

---

[53] Surah 20:102–104.
[54] Surah 79:42–46.
[55] Surah 25:17–19.
[56] Surah 21:47.
[57] Surah 21:104.
[58] Surah 5:119.

intercede for another on the Day of Judgment because each person must be held accountable for his or her own actions.[59]

The obedient will be placed in heaven and the disobedient condemned to hell. Heaven is described frequently in the Qur'an as a garden that resembles Eden, with beautiful fountains and flowing rivers, a place of peace, security, abundance, and rest.[60] Heaven will be a place where no vanity exists and the temperature is neither too hot nor too cold.[61] The Qur'an states that those who reside in heaven will not experience fatigue or sickness. It also suggests maidens or virgins will assist or serve the residents of heaven.[62] Some Muslims have suggested a sexual connection with these texts, while other Muslims are appalled by the notion that sex will be part of the heavenly realm. Islamic tradition also divides those in heaven into two categories. Those nearest to Allah will enter the Garden of Bliss where they will be served, have no pain, be fed well, be rewarded for their deeds on earth, and live in peace with Allah. The Companions of the Right Hand will live among the shade of the garden trees, have fruit in abundance, and be equal in age.[63]

Those not entering heaven, the Companions of the Left Hand, will experience the blast of fire from hell. They will be placed in boiling water, be in shades of black smoke with nothing to refresh or please them, and drink like diseased camels raging with thirst from boiling water.[64] Hell is

---

[59] Surah 20:109, 112.
[60] Surah 15:45–48.
[61] Surah 36:56–60.
[62] Surah 38:49–53.
[63] Surah 56:11–38.
[64] Surah 56:41–56.

described as a bottomless pit and a place for those who took religion to be amusement.[65] Those in hell will receive a mark that identifies them as unbelievers.[66] The residents of hell will plead for destruction, but those with stained hearts will continue to experience the justice of their rejection of Allah.[67]

Summary

The Qur'an's organization makes a systematic study difficult. One must search through many different chapters to discover the Qur'anic teaching on the nature of Allah, humanity, et cetera. Many Muslims suggest that the Qur'an was never intended to provide a theological description of Allah, but rather a plan of action for humanity. One can learn about Allah in the Qur'an, but because Allah is beyond human comprehension, the Qur'anic laws are concrete ways to worship, obey, and live out the will of God for the individual and for the Muslim community. The Qur'an describes Allah's attempt to proclaim the way to live in peace with Allah and with others. These words of wisdom were given to the Arabian people through the Apostle Muhammad, but they were meant for all of humanity. The Qur'an suggests that Muhammad is not creating a new religion but restoring the religion intended from the time of Adam and for all of human existence. Some of the characters and stories of the Qur'an are similar to those found in the Bible, but often the stories use similar characters and have different out-comes than the ones found in the Judeo-Christian Scriptures. The Qur'an is viewed as the inerrant, unchangeable revelation of Allah. The role of the

---

[65] Surah 2:9–11.
[66] Surah 55:35–44.
[67] Surah 25:13–14.

Qur'an is actually quite similar to the role of Jesus in Christianity. For Muslims, the Qur'an is the clearest picture of Allah that exists in the world today. For the Christian, Jesus is the clearest picture of God that exists today.

The Qur'an provides the blueprint for a Muslim theocracy with Allah as the absolute authority and with earthly leaders serving as Allah's *khalipha* or representatives. Because the Qur'an does not deal directly with every possible circumstance, Muslims sought guidance from other sources to help shape their understanding of Islamic law and life. Chapter 6 will focus on the development and implementation of Islamic law, but first one must gain insight into the various groups of Islam.

Chapter 4

A PICTURE OF
ISLAMIC GROUPS

A Search for Unity Amid Diversity

Following the death of Muhammad, the communities that he had united began to falter. Four major groups gave voice to the concerns facing the Muslim community following the death of their prophet. The early converts from Mecca, or the Companions, were highly respected as a group because they endured the years of persecution in Mecca and held many important positions of leadership by Muhammad's appointment. The converts from Medina represent a second group who were instrumental in helping Islam become a military power. This group had a voice, but not as strong as that of the Companions of Muhammad. Those who insisted that Ali should now lead the Muslim community, or the Legitimatists, were a small but vocal group. The Meccan aristocrats (Umayyads) who were the last group to convert to Islam were not accustomed to sharing leadership with others outside their own clan. From chapter 2, we remember that Muhammad came from the Hashim clan of the tribe of Quraysh, whereas the Umayyads represented a different and sometimes rival clan. These groups discussed the need for someone to take the mantle of leadership in order to maintain the reforms of Muhammad. The leader of the

Muslim community would take the title "Caliph," usually translated "viceroy" or "successor." The Caliph would serve to secure order throughout Muslim lands and enforce the laws provided in the Qur'an and the traditions of Muhammad (Sunnah). Handling the public funds brought in through taxation and the zakat are also duties administered by the Caliph and those around him. The qualifications for the Caliph include being a male; being a freedman; being sane and of age; having the normal physical capacities; having knowledge of divine law; having a good moral life and being just; being a descendant of the Quraysh tribe; being a capable leader in war; and being capable of discharging the necessary administrative duties.[1]

The respect given to those earlier believers from Mecca and to the companions of Muhammad led to Abu Bakr's selection as the first Caliph. The second Caliph, Umar, was also from the group of early Meccan believers. Not all the groups approved of these choices, and seeds of discontent germinated. Those who believed Ali was the only legitimate choice, often called the Legitimatists, held that the leader of the Muslim community should be a blood relative of Muhammad. Since Muhammad did not have any surviving sons, the closest male blood relative of Muhammad was Ali, his first cousin and son-in-law. The Legitimatists opposed the appointment of the first

---

[1] See Thomas Arnold and Alfred Guillaume, eds., *The Legacy of Islam* (London: Oxford University Press, 1931) 296; H. A. R. Gibb and Harold Bowen, *Islamic Society and the West: A Study of the Impact of Western Civilization on Moslem Culture in the Near East* (London: Oxford University Press, 1950) vol. 1, pt. 1, p. 28; and Erwin I. J. Rosenthal, *Studies Semitica*, vol. 2, *Islamic Themes* (Cambridge: Cambridge University Press, 1971).

two Caliphs because they were not close blood relatives of Muhammad. This group would later separate from the other groups and become known as the Shi'ites.

The discontent of the Legitimatists continued to grow during the reign of Uthman, the third Caliph or leader of the Muslim community. Uthman was a member of the Umayyad clan and represented the last group to accept Islam. Although Uthman was a son-in-law of Muhammad, he proved to be fiercely loyal to his own clan to the point of alienating the other groups. He appointed members of his clan to key posts throughout the Muslim world. The clan that represented the aristocrats of Mecca now enjoyed the growing wealth and power associated with the expansion of the Muslim world. One key appointment during Uthman's rule was the selection of his cousin Mu'awiya to be governor of Syria. From Damascus, Mu'awiya gained power and influence that would eventually shake the Islamic world.

The Legitimatists finally achieved their goal when Ali became the fourth Caliph or leader of the Muslim community. Ali's appointment, while viewed as a great victory for one group, proved to be problematic for the Umayyads who held key appointments and had gained much military power. Ali attempted to appease the Umayyads, resulting in the emergence of a fifth group called the Kharijites. The Kharijites were Muslims who believed Ali had compromised the integrity of the Caliphate and the Muslim community. Eventually most Muslims credited this group with the assassination of Ali.

The instability created during Ali's reign and following his death led to the establishment of the first empire or kingdom in Islam, the Umayyad Empire. Now in control of the Muslim world, the Umayyads established the hereditary principle for the Caliphate. The one group that continued to fight the authority were the Legitimatists, who insisted that Ali's sons were the only legitimate leaders of the Muslim community. Although the following section briefly describes the Sunni as the traditional Muslim group, the transformation of the Legitimatists into the Shi'ites is addressed soon thereafter.

The Sunni

Three of the groups (Companions, Medinans, and Umayyads) became known as Sunni because they accepted the authority of the Qur'an and the Sunnah of the prophet. The Sunni represent the majority of all Muslims today and are proponents of traditional, orthodox Islam. Recognizing the importance of the Muslim community, these three groups trusted the community's judgment in selecting Abu Bakr to serve as the first leader of the community after Muhammad's death. They often refer to the first four Caliphs as the Rightly Guided Caliphs because they served as both political and religious leaders of the community. By the time of the Umayyad Empire, the role of Caliph became primarily a political one, and the religious leadership of the community fell to religious specialists or *ulama*. They believed the community could be trusted to make the right choice of the Caliph through consensus or *ijma*. They held to the notion that the community would never agree on an error, and therefore they could be trusted to follow the leadership of God in making such important decisions. The Sunni also believed that the divine revelation ended with Muhammad; thus, the role of the religious leaders was to secure that members of the Islamic community followed the revelations of the Qur'an that were revealed through Muhammad. They believe that the Caliphs or leaders of the community were subject to error and can be replaced if they failed to maintain the demands of the Islamic law. The political and religious leadership provide guidance to the Islamic community. Over time "Caliph" became the name given to the political leaders of the community, and "Imam" was the name given to those who provided counsel on religious matters. A mosque serviced each portion of the community, and an Imam led each mosque.

The duties of the Caliph included the protection of religion from external and internal attack; administration of justice; maintenance of order and peace and protection of property; execution of punishments for civil and religious crimes; fortification of borders; prosecution of jihad; tax collection; and religious gifts.[2] The Caliph functioned as the leader of the community, but not with the same authority of Muhammad. The Caliph was to represent both spiritual maturity and the political savvy necessary to rule the Muslim community.

Sunni Muslims hold that the Qur'an teaches that no one can intercede or mediate between God and human beings. All human beings are accountable to God for their actions and their beliefs. They do hold to the notion that a messiah or mahdi will take part in the Day of Judgment, yet Sunni Muslims differ on the identity of the messiah and the role that messiah is to play.

---

[2] See al-Mawardi's list in Andrea Farsakh, "A Comparison of the Sunni Caliphate and the Shi'i Imamate," *Muslim World* 59:2 (April 1969): 129.

The Shi'ites

The Shi'ites believed that only blood relatives of Muhammad were legitimate leaders of the Muslim community. They considered Ali to be the obvious choice to lead the community because he was his closest male blood relative following Muhammad's death (first cousin). By implication, this meant that Abu Bakr, Umar, and Uthman were all illegitimate leaders of the Muslim community of faith. The Shi'ite stance proved to be unpopular with the remaining Muslims because they viewed most of the companions of Muhammad as not being worthy of the mantle of leadership.

The Shi'ites began primarily as a political movement. They believed that Ali represented both the political and religious ideals of Islam. Shi'ites and Sunni were probably theologically very compatible early in Muslim history. The Shi'ite opposition to the Umayyads brought them much persecution. Eventually, though, the group that identified themselves as the Abbasids used the Shi'ites and other groups that desired a change in leadership to overthrow the Umayyads and establish the Abbasid Empire. The Shi'ite movement remained mostly political until the ninth century when the unique religious ideas began to emerge.

From the ninth century until today, the theological developments of the Shi'ites separated them from the remainder of the Muslim community labeled Sunni. Sunni or traditional Muslims view some of these theological differences as dangerous and even heretical. Although many of these ideas may predate the ninth century, they emerged then as distinctive doctrines that would shape the identity and nature of the Shi'ite movement to this day.

The Shi'ites not only hold that Ali was the legitimate leader of the Muslim community following Muhammad's death, but they point to traditions in which Muhammad named Ali as his successor.[3] The Shi'ites hold to the notion that Ali is the most excellent Muslim after Muhammad. They believed that their political leader must also be their spiritual leader. Instead of using the language of Caliph and Caliphate, the Shi'ites use the terms "Imam" and "Imamate." The Imam must be a descendant of Muhammad through Ali and his wife Fatimah, the daughter of Muhammad. Most Shi'ites (Isna Asharai or "Twelvers") believe that twelve of these Imams have existed in human history, while others believe the number to be only seven ("Seveners" or "Isma'ilis") or five ("Fivers" or "Zaydis").[4] The Twelvers are a majority in Iran, Iraq, and Bahrain with minority populations in Afghanistan, Lebanon, Pakistan, India, Syria, Turkey, Saudi Arabia, Yemen, the former Soviet Union, and the Gulf States. The Zaydis are the second largest group of Shi'ites and are primarily found in Yemen. The smallest Shi'ite group is the Isma'ilis, whose members can be found in India, Central Asia, Iran, Syria, and East Africa.[5]

Unlike the Sunni Muslims, the Shi'ites do not believe that leadership of the Muslim community can be entrusted to

---

[3] See al-Mawardi's list in Farsakh, "A Comparison," *Muslim World* 59:2, p. 54 for a description of the different Shi'ite traditions pointing to Muhammad's naming of Ali as his successor.

[4] For a biography of each of the twelve imams, see chapter 3 of Moojan Momen's *An Introduction to Shi'i Islam* (New Haven: Yale University Press, 1985).

[5] See "Shi'ism," in Cyril Glassé, *The Concise Encyclopedia of Islam* (New York: HarperCollins Publishers, 1989) 364–70.

consensus (ijma). Shi'ites believe God must appoint the Imam
and that the Imam continues to receive revelations to assist the
Muslim community to honor God's desires. They believe these
religious leaders can use creative reasoning or effort (*ijtihad*)
that was later forbidden by some of the Sunni legal schools.
Shi'ites trust in the decisions of the Imams because they
believe Imams are sinless (*nass*) and their authority is beyond
question. The Imam serves as the Divine Light (*nur*) or the
Shadow of God in the world. The Shi'ites also believe that the
world cannot exist without the presence of the Imam. Because
the world must have the Imam, the Shi'ites hold that the last
Imam did not die but went into hiding until the Day of
Judgment. They also believe the Imam will serve as an
intercessor or mediator between God and all Shi'ites on the
Day of Judgment. According to the twelvers, the last Imam
disappeared in the ninth century, and since that time religious
leaders called Mujtahidin have functioned as the
representatives of the same guidance in the absence of a visible
Imam. The highest-ranking Mujtahidin are called Ayatollah. In
recent history, the Iranian Revolution was led by Ayatollah
Khomeini. High-ranking religious leaders or Ayatollahs
continue to lead Iran.

Shi'ite traditions detail the duties of the Imam as having
absolute authority over men as ordained by God; the witness of
the people with God; responsibility for the gates of Allah; the
road and guide to God; the repository of God's knowledge;
interpreter of God's revelations; and the pillar of God's unity.[6]
The duties of the Imam point primarily to spiritual guidance,

---

[6] See al-Qummi's list in Farsakh, "A Comparison," *Muslim World*
59:2, p. 130.

whereas the duties often listed for the Caliph focus heavily on social and political actions.

Two other interesting characteristics of the Shi'ites are the roles of suffering and deceit. The suffering concept emerged in recognition of the martyrdom of Ali's son Husayn at Karbala. His willingness to face a certain death has shown that persecution has and is a constant companion of the Shi'ites around the world and they must share Husayn's courage. The martyrdom of Husayn is reenacted each year in what is sometimes called the Passion Play in Iran, where Shi'ites beat or wound themselves in the street as an expression of mourning. Because suffering and persecution is part of the price for being a minority, Shi'ites are allowed to use deceit (*taqiyya*) to deny any connection to Shi'ite doctrines in order to prevent persecution.[7] Today Shi'ites represent about 10 percent of the worldwide Muslim population.[8]

The Sufi

Virtually all Muslims today identify themselves as either Sunni or Shi'ite. Yet, without exploring the Sufi or mystic movement within Islam, one misses an important force in Islamic history. The word *sufi* likely can be traced to the Arabic word for wool, "suf," since many of the early Sufis dressed in plain woolen robes to reflect their desire to choose a simple, pious life. Sufis trace their traditions back to Muhammad through his cousin and son-in-law, Ali. Sufi tradition holds that Muhammad passed on the Sufi traditions to Ali, who passed them on to his

---

[7] Farsakh, "A Comparison," *Muslim World* 59:2, pp. 137–38.

[8] For an estimated survey on the numbers of Shi'ites by country, see Momen, *Introduction to Shi'i Islam*, 282.

sons. Since then, Sufi traditions have been passed on through history down to the Sufis who exist today.

The history of Sufism is not easy to trace. Although the traditions are believed to go back to Muhammad, according to the Sufis, the Sufi movements probably did not emerge until about the twelfth century. The Shi'ites became powerful politically during the tenth and eleventh centuries; however, Turkish forces tumbled the Shi'ite power that placed them once again as a persecuted people. Because the Sufis have great respect for Ali and most of the Imams revered by the Shi'ites, they found a connection with the Shi'ites. A popular theory is that the Sufi movement emerged to fill the void left by the absence of the Shi'ite teachings.[9] Yet, the differences between the two groups led to persecution of the Sufis when the Shi'ites became predominant in Iran. One source of conflict was the fact that Shi'ites held that the Imams were the only reliable source of revelation following the death of Muhammad, whereas the Sufis believed their spiritual masters were as reliable as the Imams because they were part of the great chain of transmission that came directly from Muhammad.[10] These Sufi leaders were often called Poles of the Universe because they held the knowledge that came directly from God to Muhammad. A second source of conflict was their notion of existential monism (explained below), which conflicted with the Shi'ite concept of absolute monotheism. Although attempts were made to bring Sufi and Shi'ite ideas closer together, the Shi'ites and later the Sunnis looked with great suspicion on the Sufi movement. In the twentieth century, Modernists criticized Sufis, blaming them for the backward socioeconomic status of

---

[9] Momen, *Introduction to Shi'i Islam*, 208.
[10] Ibid., 209.

Muslim countries in the world. Participants in Muslim reform movements also blamed Sufis for trying to undermine the orthodoxy of Islam. To understand the Sufis and their impact on Islam, one must explore some of the unique beliefs and practices of those who follow the Sufi way of life.

Cyril Glassé defines Sufism as "the science of the direct knowledge of God; its doctrines and methods are derived from the Koran and Islamic revelation."[11] One of the key ingredients of the Sufi tradition is initiation into the Sufi order. The Sufi guide must determine the worthiness of the potential student. One could argue that a person does not find Sufism, but Sufis finds qualified persons. According to Sufi tradition, Muhammad was initiated by the angel Gabriel when he received the first revelations of the Qur'an. This implies that God, through Gabriel, considered Muhammad to be a worthy student. Muhammad then, according to Sufi tradition, initiated Ali, who then initiated his sons, and that line continues in modern-day Sufis. A second key principle of the Sufis is that the only way to gain access to this unique relationship with God is to be taught by a master.[12] This method of passing down knowledge from teacher to student is commonly found in Christianity through the concept of discipleship. Hinduism and Buddhism also use this method of the teacher (guru) passing important knowledge down to worthy students. The Greek philosopher Socrates used a similar method, and today this dialogical, personal teaching style is called the Socratic method.

---

[11] Glassé, *Encyclopedia*, 375.

[12] For a summary of the characteristics of Sufism, see Carl W. Ernst, *Sufism: An Essential Introduction to the Philosophy and Practice of the Mystical Tradition of Islam* (Boston: Shambhala Publications, Inc., 1997) 27–31.

Another important characteristic of the Sufis is the desire to free oneself from the distractions of the world in order to gain intimacy with God. This spiritual intoxication with God shares common traits with Christian, Jewish, and Eastern forms of mysticism. The desire is not merely to know about God, but to have a direct, personal experience with God. The result of this experience should be the development of a selfless person who reflects humility, love, and morality. In order to experience God, one must remove oneself, an act that humbles the person and enables him both to love God and serve God faithfully.

The Sufi teaching resulting in the most persecution is the principle of existential monism. Orthodox Islam holds dear the belief that no God exists except God. This principle of absolute monotheism has been one of the cornerstones of Islamic belief since the earliest revelations of the Qur'an. The principle of monism holds that every person is a small extension of God, who created the universe and all persons who dwell in the world. Some Greek and Hindu philosophies also support the principle of monism. Monism allows the individual to connect with God in a direct, mystical experience because the person is actually an extension of God. Some may refer to this religious perspective as pantheism. A Sufi may choose one of three paths to arrive at this direct experience with God: action, devotion, or knowledge.[13] Hindus, too, use similar paths to God as part of their religious experience. The path of action means that the Sufi has chosen to act selflessly in dealing with others. The path of devotion focuses on devoting oneself to knowing God and submitting to the will of God in

---

[13] Glassé, *Encyclopedia*, 379.

all one does and says. Those who choose the path of knowledge seek an experiential knowledge that cannot be gained from books alone. The understanding of knowledge is similar to the understanding exhibited by the Gnostics during first century

One other characteristic that causes difficulty for Sufis is the relationship to the local community. Islam historically forbids monasticism, yet many Sufis became frustrated with the hypocrisy of their Muslim community and chose to isolate themselves physically from the rest of the community. The isolation increased the Muslim community's suspicion of the Sufi one must remember how important the concept of community is for the Muslim. They were also criticized for drawing many of their ideas from the Greek philosophers Aristotle and Plato.

Sufis usually organize into groups that share a common teacher. These groups sometimes develop their own unique styles and emphases. Some of these groups gain knowledge through reading the poetry of famous Sufi writers such as al-Rumi or Omar Khayyam. Some groups, like the whirling dervishes, gain unity with God through music and dance. The common goal of all Muslims is to have a direct experience with God so that they might be able to honor God with their words and deeds. Extreme Sufis may seek to unite with God by eating glass, piercing the body with knives or hooks, or enduring some other form of self-inflicted pain. The famous writer al-Ghazali wrote the following words about his exploration of Sufism:

...the gist of the doctrine [of the Sufis] lies in overcoming the appetites of the flesh and getting rid of its evil dispositions and vile qualities, so that the heart may be cleared of all but God; and the means of clearing it is dhikr Allah (remembrance of God] and concentration of every thought upon Him....

Worldly interests encompassed me on every side. Even my work as a teacher—the best thing I was engaged in—seemed unimportant and useless in view of the life hereafter. When I considered the intention of my teaching, I perceived that instead of doing it for God's sake alone I had no motive but the desire for glory and reputation. I realized that I stood on the edge of a precipice and would fall into Hellfire unless I set about to mend my ways.... Conscious of my helplessness and having surrendered my will entirely, I took refuge with God as a man in sore trouble who has no resource left.[14]

Today Sufism is alive and active, but what it means to be a Sufi has altered over the years. Some Sufis seek to dialogue with persons from other religions who share in some common religious experiences. Some consider Sufism to mean so many different things to so many different people that it has lost some of its fervor as a religious reform movement. The famous Sufi quote describes the current situation of Sufism: "In the beginning Sufism was a reality without a name; today it is a name without a reality."[15]

---

[14] Ibid.
[15] Ibid., 376.

Summary

Although other groups could be listed, the Sunnis, Shi'ites, and Sufis represent the three most common groupings of Muslims. The Sunnis and Shi'ites are distinguished by their teachings and practices, except for those Shi'ites who are living in a hostile environment. Sufis, on the other hand, can emerge from either a Shi'ite or Sunni background. Because Sufis strive for humility, one may have a difficult time finding persons who openly identify themselves as Sufis. The next chapter provides a synopsis of Islamic history in order to demonstrate how these groups interacted in the unfolding of the story of Islam.

Chapter 5

A PICTURE OF
ISLAMIC HISTORY

Age of the Companions

The four major groups that gave voice to the community's concerns following the death of Muhammad were the early converts from Mecca, those from Medina who converted to Islam, those who believed that Ali should now lead the Muslim community, and the Meccan aristocrats (Umayyads) who were the last to convert to Islam (as discussed in chapter 4). These groups discussed who should serve as the successor of Muhammad. After much discussion, Abu Bakr was chosen to lead the Muslim community, in spite of the strong advocacy of Ali by one of the four groups. Abu Bakr, Muhammad's father-in-law, was one of the first male converts and probably also his closest friend. Abu Bakr helped the people understand the role of Muhammad while the community mourned his passing. These oft-quoted words of Abu Bakr were timely for the grieving Muslim community:

> O People! If anyone among you worshiped Muham-
> mad, let him know that Muhammad is dead. But those
> who worship Allah, let him know that He lives and
> will never die. Let all of us recall the words of the

Qur'an. It says, 'Muhammad is only a Messenger of Allah. There have been Messengers before him. What then, will you turn back from Islam, if he dies or is killed?"[1]

Abu Bakr successfully brought a sense of unity back to the community, even though the differences between these four groups would eventually cause the community to splinter. In his first address to the Muslim community, Bakr told the people,

> I have been given authority over you, and I am not the best of you. If I do well, help me; and if I do wrong, set me right. Sincere regard for truth is loyalty and disregard for truth is treachery. The weak amongst you shall be strong with me until I have secured his rights, if God wills; and the strong amongst you shall be weak with me until I have wrestled from him the rights of others, if God wills. Obey me so long as I obey God and His Messenger (Muhammad). But if I disobey God and His Messenger, you owe me no obedience. Arise for your prayer, God have mercy upon you.[2]

Abu Bakr's desire to serve God was displayed when he used his wealth to free slaves who were persecuted because of their Islamic beliefs. He also had the reputation for being able

---

[1] Hamzah Qassem, "Abu Bakr As-Siggiq: The Truthful companion," http://quraan.con/index.aspx?8tabid=35&artid'66.

[2] *Abu Bakr, The First Caliph (632–634 C.E.),* "Caliph Abu Bakr's First Address," http://www.cyberistan.org/islamic/abubakr.html.

to interpret dreams.[3] He served as Caliph of the Muslim community from 632 until his death in 634. On his deathbed, Abu Bakr appointed Umar to be the next Caliph.

Umar was known as a passionate, strong-willed person. Initially, he fiercely opposed Islam as he discovered that his sister and brother-in-law had become Muslims. He came to their home to rebuke them for their indiscretion and instead converted to Islam himself.[4] The same passion he used to oppose Islam then became a passion for Islam. As Caliph, he expanded the territory ruled by Islam at a remarkable rate that led Cyril Glassé to write,

> Under his rule the Islamic Empire expanded with almost miraculous speed, and it is fair to say that it was 'Umar who, after the Prophet (Muhammad), was most influential in molding the Islamic state, and in determining its nature....
>
> All later movements that attempted the restoration of a "pure Islamic state" looked back to the Caliphate of 'Umar as the ideal model, with the exception of the Twelve-Imam Shi'ites, for whom all rulers not of the family of 'Ali are usurpers, especially the first three Caliphs.[5]

Umar developed a strategy that allowed him to expand the territory of Islam with minimal disruption to the conquered communities. Part of the strategy was to allow Christians,

---

[3] The Sahih Bukhar Collection of Hadith highlights Abu Bakr's ability to interpret dreams (Book 87: Interpretation of Dreams).

[4] Glassé, *Encyclopedia*, 407.

[5] Glassé, *Encyclopedia*, 407-408.

Jews, and Zoroastrians to continue practicing their religions if they would agree to pay a tax that would secure their protection from hostile enemies.[6] His system allowed for expansion and reduced the chances that an uprising would follow their enemies' defeat. He allowed the victors to take some material possessions as booty, but the land remained the property of the local community. Lapidus suggests that the Muslim community was a political expansion of Arab territories rather than a missionary campaign to convert the world to Islam.[7] He suggests that the conversion of a person to Islam might actually create problems because the individual could then be eligible for status and rights that would have to be shared by the Arab Muslims.

Umar was the first to pay salaries to those who led in prayer (Imams) and those who called the community to prayer (muezzins). The positive side of this policy was that religious leaders received a politically recognized status, but the downside of his public treasury was that those who could least afford to pay were taxed. Peasants, workers, and merchants bore the brunt of the tax burden so that religious and political leaders could devote full attention to their duties.

Umar also inaugurated the practice of public beatings for drinking alcohol. This practice was reinstated in Chechnya in 1996 to punish the Muslims who sold vodka to Russian soldiers during the First Chechnyan War (1994–1996). The reinstatement supports Glassé's claim that those trying to establish a "true Islamic state" are using Umar's policies as a model for the contemporary world. A disgruntled Persian slave

---

[6] Ira Lapidus, *A History of Islamic Societies* (New York: Cambridge University Press, 1988) 43.

[7] Ibid.

stabbed Umar to death because Umar ignored his complaint
against his master, the governor of Basra (Iraq). Before he died,
Umar appointed a council or *shura* whose responsibility would
be the appointment of the next Caliph. One of the council
members became the third Caliph, Uthman.

Uthman was the first Caliph from the Meccan aristocratic
group called the Umayyad, whose members strongly opposed
Muhammad before finally accepting Islam. The first half of
Uthman's reign proved to be peaceful, but he sowed the seeds
of discontent by showing favoritism to the Meccan aristocrats.
Until this time, the Muslims from Medina and the early Meccan converts to Islam were the dominant force in the Muslim
community. Uthman appointed other Umayyads to positions
of leadership throughout Muslim lands. One appointment that
would shape future events was that of Mu'awiya as governor of
Syria. The rights and privileges experienced by these aristocrats in pre-Islamic Arabia disappeared when Mecca fell to the
Muslims in Medina, but Uthman worked diligently to restore
them to his Umayyad brethren.[8] Uthman's policies alienated
the Meccan companions, Medinan converts, and the Legitimatists and led to several revolts that took place in the latter
half of his reign. The lack of support he experienced in Medina
due to his nepotism and the increase in the revolts resulted in
his assassination in 656 by 500 Arabs from Fustat (now Cairo,
Egypt).[9]

While most of his kinsmen converted when Mecca was
handed over to Muhammad in 630, Uthman was one of the
first Umayyad converts to Islam. His conversion occurred as he

---

[8] Ibid., 56.

[9] Cyril Glassé, *The Concise Encyclopedia of Islam* (New York:
HarperCollins Publishers, 1989) 412.

was awakened by a voice while returning from a journey to Syria. The voice told him that Ahmad (another name for Muhammad) had come to Mecca. Uthman sought the council of Abu Bakr, who introduced him to Muhammad.[10] The two formed a special connection because Uthman would marry two of Muhammad's daughters.

Uthman's most important positive contribution was his compilation of the Qur'an so that he could put the authoritative text in writing. This text was then sent throughout the Islamic ruled lands as the standard text of the Qur'an. This edition of the Qur'an is still used today.

Following the murder of Uthman, Ali became the fourth Caliph to rule the Muslim community. Ali's appointment was met with glee by those who believed him to be the first legitimate Caliph who shared a bloodline with Muhammad. As one of the first two male converts to Islam, Ali was also Muhammad's first cousin and husband to Muhammad's daughter Fatimah. Unfortunately, Ali could not have chosen a more difficult time to serve as Caliph.

Ali was always with Muhammad, and though he was one of the prophet's youngest companions, he gained a reputation for being a person of character and great spiritual maturity. Some Muslims believed Muhammad would name Ali as his successor, but Sunni Muslims hold that Ali died before this could be completed.[11] The crisis of his reign began almost the moment he took the mantle of leadership. The Umayyads demanded vengeance on the assassin who killed one of their

---

[10] Ibid.

[11] See Moojan Momen, *An Introduction to Shi'i Islam* (Yale University Press, 1985) 15–16 for an elaboration of the time when Muhammad was to name Ali as his successor.

own. Because Ali did not act in a way that satisfied the Umayyads, many of the group's leaders no longer recognized his authority. The governor of Syria, Mu'awiya, demanded that Uthman's death be avenged and accused Ali of aiding Uthman's killers. Mu'awiya began to stir the flames of rebellion against Ali. Others joined the rebellion for a variety of reasons, and division plagued Ali's time as Caliph. The Umayyads, who came to enjoy a great deal of power and influence during the reign of Uthman, were not willing to give up their positions when Ali attempted to appoint persons to posts held by the Umayyads.

Ali had a reputation for being honest and forthright, which made him highly respected as a religious leader but vulnerable as a political leader. Ali took actions simply for political expedience, which made recruitment for the rebellion easier because Mu'awiya was comfortable with making political deals. Ali decided to move his headquarters from Medina to Kufa in what is today Iraq. Mu'awiya moved his troops toward Kufa to challenge Ali's troops. They fought at Siffin, and the battle proved to be a draw. Ali sent a negotiator to work out an agreement with Mu'awiya. Some portray Ali as a coward for trying to negotiate, but others suggest he made the best available choice. Some of Ali's troops would not accept the agreement with Mu'awiya and turned their wrath toward Ali. This group of soldiers, called the Kharijites, became a greater threat to Ali than the Umayyads. Although Ali was able to defeat the Kharijites in battle, one of them succeeded in assassinating Ali in 661 (see chapter 4). Mu'awiya successfully overpowered Ali's two sons, Hasan and Husayn, to become the next Caliph.

Umayyad Empire (661–750, 756–1031)

Mu'awiya gained control of the Islamic world and eventually made Damascus the capital of the newly founded empire. Damascus was a natural choice since Mu'awiya had already been serving as the governor of Syria. Syria had once been under the control of the Byzantine Empire or Eastern Empire, with Constantinople as its capital. Mu'awiya chose an administrative structure that seemed to mirror the Christian Byzantine model. He also established the precedent that the Caliphate should be passed on to the sons of the Caliph. His own son, Yazd, became Caliph following Mu'awiya's death.

Not only did the Umayyad administration reveal a Byzantine influence, but they also emulated the lifestyles of the Byzantine rulers. Music and gambling, which Muhammad forbade, reappeared during the Umayyad Caliphate. Horse racing and other past-times common in pre-Islamic Arabia were renewed during the time of the Umayyad Empire. Muslim historians usually consider the Umayyad Empire as a step backward for Islam. Many activities of Arabia that were considered immoral by Muhammad, such as drinking alcohol, were reestablished. Arab values and Arabs themselves enjoyed privileges, but non-Arab converts to Islam were often considered second-class citizens. This treatment of the non-Arab populations would eventually lead to the overthrow of the Umayyad Empire.

Key events during the time of the Umayyad Empire include the building of the Dome of the Rock mosque in Jerusalem in 691, the entry into Europe via Spain in 711, and the Battle of Poitiers that halted the Muslim advance before it could enter France in 732. Important developments during this time included the spread of Arab culture and the Arab language wherever the empire expanded. When the Umayyads established themselves in Spain, Arabic became the predominant language of the areas controlled by the Muslims. After the Umayyad Empire was defeated in 750 in Syria, it reemerged as an empire centered in Cordova, Spain, from 756 to 1031.

The fall of the Umayyad Empire came at the hands of the Abbasids, a group that drew support from the Shi'ites and the non-Arab Muslims who sought to gain an equal footing with the Arab Muslims.

Abbasid Empire (750–1258, 1261–1517)

The Abbasids claimed to be descendants of Abbas, the uncle of the prophet Muhammad. They used the Shi'ite political rhetoric and the poor treatment of non-Arabs to end the Umayyad Empire. The Abbasids built their capital city on the Tigris River and named it Baghdad. The Abbasids sought to make Islam a world religion without showing preference to those of Arab origins. The Abbasid period gave the world *The Book of One Thousand and One Nights* that included stories about Alladin, Ali Baba and the Forty Thieves, and Sinbad the Sailor. Stories of genies, magic bottles, flying carpets, have inspired films, music, and games around the world..

The political administration of the Abbasids attempted to restore a more orthodox Islamic administration. They appointed non-Arab citizens to key positions that satisfied those who had helped lead the revolution against the Umayyads. Although they used non-Muslims in the government, and in spite of the Shi'ite contribution to their victory, the Abbasids dedicated themselves to restore orthodoxy, which led to a separation between the Abbasid Caliphs and the Shi'ites.

Shortly after the Abbasids gained control of the empire, the Shi'ites endured increasing persecution. The Shi'ites organized rebellions in Basra, Kufa, Mecca, and Medina. They became the anti-establishment movement against the Abbasids. Persians gained key positions, and their influence could be felt in many different areas of life. One custom that came from the Persians was the vizerate, a system by which the King (Caliph) would appoint a trusted political advisor to assist in making significant decisions for the empire. In the latter days of the empire, the vizier became the true power. Eventually many Persians joined the Shi'ites to combat the Abbasids that would eventually lead to Iran being primarily a Shi'ite dominated country.

The Abbasid Empire introduced a period of great learning, political expansion, and religious fervor, leading many Muslims to consider this era as the Golden Age of Islam. Many of the great philosophical works of Plato and Aristotle were discovered and translated into Arabic. Because of the translation efforts of Muslim scholars, the Arabic translations, which were later found in Spain, gave Europe access to these important writings. Algebra, paraffin for kerosene lamps, and research on smallpox and measles are but a few advances that emerged during the time of the Abbasid Empire.

The Crusades of Christian Europe occurred during the time of Abbasid Empire existed (1095, 1145, 1187, 1198, 1218, 1229). The Crusaders marched into Muslim lands wearing uniforms and carrying shields that sported a cross, aiming to take back holy lands and relics. For this reason, the cross continues to be a negative image for most Muslims. (Chapter 10 addresses the impact of the Crusades.)

Important events for the Abbasid Empire include the expansion of the Muslim presence into Central Asia in 751, the loss of Jerusalem to the Crusaders in 1099 and its restoration to Muslim hands by Saladin the Great in 1187, and the loss of Jerusalem in 1229 and its recapture in 1244/45.

The fall of the Abbasid Empire came at the hands of the Mongols, led by the grandson of Genghis Khan, who destroyed Baghdad and ended the Golden Age of Islam. The surviving members of the Abbasids fled to Egypt and reestablished a shadow empire centered in Cairo. The real power behind the reestablished Abbasid Empire was a military group called the Mamluks that was composed of former slaves from Turkey and Central Asia.

Fatimid Empire (909–1171)

Individuals who claimed to be descendants of Muhammad through his daughter Fatimah established the Fatimid Empire. Many Muslim scholars consider this group's claim questionable, although some hold that the link to Fatimah is at least possible. The Fatimid Empire was the only Shi'ite empire in the history of Islam. The founders of the empire used the Shi'ite concept of the Mahdi or messiah and used a Muslim tradition or Hadith to declare that the messiah would be a descendant of Fatimah. To secure their rightful place as leaders of the Muslim community, they referred to the empire as the Fatimid Empire after the daughter of Muhammad. They became established in North Africa in 909 and finally took control of Egypt in 969.

The Fatimid Empire had many parallels with the Abbasid Empire in Baghdad. The Fatimids, like the Abbasids, built a city—Cairo—and made it the capital of their empire. Like the

Abbasids, they excelled in intellectual pursuits, and their legacy points to a period of intense learning. The greatest remnant of the Fatimid contribution to learning is the Al-Azhar University in Cairo. Today this mosque and university is one of the most prestigious in the Muslim world.

Like the Abbasids, the Fatimids used a vizerate system so that the Caliph had an advisor who assisted him with important decisions. Also like the Abbasids, the viziers became powerful enough that they served as the true leaders of the empire. For a short time, the Fatimids held possession of Syria and Palestine. Additionally, the Fatimid period was known for the great contributions made in Islamic art and philosophy. As with the Abbasids, the Turkish soldiers the Fatimids used as bodyguards eventually took control of the imperial lands.

The Fatimid Empire represented the Twelver Shi'ite tradition, yet they did not force their beliefs on the residents of the empire. They also developed interesting relationships with nearby empires. They united with the Christian Byzantine Empire to combat the growing Turkish force that jeopardized the existence of both empires. They even exchanged ambassadors.

In 1171, the Fatimid Empire fell at the hands of the famous Abbasid, Saladin the Great. The fall of the Fatimids at the hands of the Abbasids provided a short-lived victory, because the Turkish threat was building and would eventually result in the establishment of the Ottoman Empire.

Ottoman Empire (1290–1924)

The Ottoman Turks established their empire by defeating the Mongols who brought the Abbasid Empire to an end. Following their defeat of the Abbasids in Cairo, the Turks began using the title "Sultan" and later the term "Caliph" to secure power throughout the Muslim world. The Ottoman Empire was geographically the largest in Muslim history, and it represents the longest continuous Muslim empire, yet Muslim historians have not spoken fondly of this period in Islamic history. The empire stretched all the way to Austria and Romania in Europe. Vlad the Impaler, who later became known as Dracula, led the resistance against the Turks in Romania.

Key events during the time of the Ottoman Empire include the capture of Constantinople (renamed Istanbul) in 1453, the empire's expansion into southeast Asia by 1550 (Java and Borneo), the dismantling of the Ottoman Empire by the Europeans in the 1800s, and the Turkish support of Germany during World War I that sealed the empire's fate. Following World War I, Turkey won its independence through the efforts of Mustafa Kamal Ataturk, who promptly abolished the Caliphate in 1924.

Contemporary Islam

Since the collapse of the Ottoman Empire, attempts have been made to reestablish the Caliphate, but nationalism and global politics have prevented it. Muslim regions have developed into many nations that attempt to merge Islam with either communism or democracy. Chapters 8 and 9 are dedicated to the developments of contemporary Islam.

Summary

Muslim history is a story of both diversity and internal conflict. During certain periods, three different persons took the title of Caliph at the same time. Most devoted Muslims believe the true Caliphate ended when the Abbasid Empire fell and that those who came after that time were merely pretenders to the political authority that came with the title "Caliph." Chapters 8 and 9 explore movements in contemporary Islam and chapter 10 focuses on the interaction between Muslims and Christians through history.

Chapter 6

a pictuRe of
muslim law and life

To discuss Islamic law, one must go back to the life of Muhammad. From the beginning of Muhammad's ministry, personal piety was necessary to fulfill God's purpose for every human life. Chapter 2 indicates that the transformation of the Muslim community when Muhammad moved to Medina was vitally important. For the first time in Medina, the Muslims were able to openly establish a community that would be spared harsh persecution and could observe the laws revealed to them in the Qur'an. The revelations of the Qur'an that came to Muhammad during his life in Medina focused heavily on legal and social matters. In Medina, Islam transformed from an isolated religious community of Meccan Muslims into a diverse religious community with political clout.

What did it mean for the Muslims to establish a community in Medina? First, the term *ummah* was used to refer to the Meccans who had received the authority of the Qur'an and accepted Muhammad as the messenger of God. The Qur'an points to the fact that at one time, humankind was one community (Surah 10:19), but through God's word they became diverse communities. God secured a prophet to speak to each community (Surah 10:47). The Arab community, composed of Meccan converts to Islam from Muhammad's tribe, became part of the Muslim community in Medina. The Medinan community was diverse, with Muslims from both Meccan and Medinan backgrounds. A non-Quranic source called the Medina Charter shows that Medina was to be one community including the Meccan Muslims, Medinan Muslims, and Jewish tribes. The intent was for the Muslim community to coexist with the Jewish community to create a harmonious larger community. The Jewish community did not have to leave, but its members had to recognize the authority of the larger Muslim community in return for protection during a time of invasion. To explain the development of and the changes in Islamic law, the following material focuses on the six periods of Fiqh (jurisprudence) in the history of Islam.[1]

Six Periods of Islamic Jurisprudence

The Prophetic Period (610–632). The understanding of Islamic law during Muhammad's life was a fairly simple matter. The Qur'an revealed the laws all Muslims should observe, and Muhammad acted or spoke to address any life situation not covered by the Qur'an. Thus the earliest sources of Islamic law were the Qur'an and the Sunnah (words or actions) of Muhammad. During Muhammad's time in Medina, he established many laws that would be binding to all Muslims.[2] These laws represent both requirements and prohibitions for all Muslims. Although not all of the laws that became binding

---

[1] Mohammad Hashim Kamali, "Law and Society: The Interplay of Revelation and Reason in the Shariah," in *The Oxford History of Islam,* ed. John Esposito (Oxford: Oxford University Press, 1999) 100–18.

[2] See http://www.islam.com for a suggested chronology of the life of Muhammad including the years that the early Muslim laws were put in effect.

arose from the Medinan period, the majority did. Because Muhammad lived among the people, he was available to answer questions concerning Islamic law. Some of the laws established during Muhammad's lifetime were the five pillars (shahadah, salat, zakat, sawm, and hajj),[3] the law forbidding a Muslim to marry a non-Muslim, the prohibition of alcohol, dietary restrictions, tax for nonbelievers living in a Muslim state to assure their protection, and fighting in defense of the cause of Allah (jihad).[4]

The Era of the Companions (632–661). After the death of Muhammad, the Muslim community continued to follow the Islamic law established by Muhammad in Medina. The community chose a man to serve as the political and spiritual head. The period from 632–661 is often called the period of the Rightly Guided Caliphs because the four men who led the Muslim community were seen as both political and spiritual leaders. The major shift in Islamic law during this time is that none of the leaders had the status of a prophet; therefore, they did not have the level of authority recognized in Muhammad. Legal questions arose at this point that were not previously addressed in the Qur'an or in the life of Muhammad. How does one deal with legal issues without a precedent? The people used creative reasoning (*itjihad*) based on principles found in the Qur'an or in the actions of Muhammad that applied to similar contexts. The Rightly Guided Caliphs had to make decisions concerning legal questions that addressed the needs of the growing Muslim community. Legal scholars began emerging to help guide the Caliphs and to record

---

[3] See pp. 46-51 for a detailed description of the five pillars.
[4] See page 39 for a discussion of the term jihad.

decisions for posterity. During this period, Islamic jurisprudence or *fiqh* was established.[5]

Era of the Successors (661–750). The third period of Islamic law lasted from the beginning of the Umayyad Empire until its demise in 750. During this time, legal scholars continued to advise and write on legal decisions, but differences of opinions emerged. These differences led to the development of two distinctive approaches to Islamic law. One approach, found mainly in Mecca and Medina, focused on the primacy of the written sources and discouraged any form of creative reasoning.[6] The other approach, found primarily in Kufa and Basra in what is today Iraq, embraced creative reasoning whenever a clear text could not be found to address the legal situation.[7] One other development during this period was the formation of a separate Shi'ite legal school.

Era of Independent Reasoning (750–950). During the next 200 years, the primary legal schools that exist today were formed. The Maliki legal school emerged in the eighth century and is still influential in North Africa.[8] The Hanafi legal school also emerged in the eighth century and remains important for the areas once identified with the Ottoman and Moghul empires.[9] Two more schools came into existence in the ninth

---

[5] Kamali, "Law and Society," 111.

[6] Ibid., 112.

[7] Ibid.

[8] Ibid., 113 (Morocco, Algeria, Tunisia, northern Egypt, Sudan, Bahrain, and Kuwait).

[9] Ibid., 114 (Turkey, Pakistan, Jordan, Lebanon, and Afghanistan).

century: the Shafi'i legal school predominant in Egypt and the Hanabali legal school that dominates Saudi Arabia.[10]

Also formed during this period was the *ulama*. The ulama represented the religious scholars and leaders of the community who served as an advisory group to the Muslim leader at the time. The power of the religious leaders in the community continues today in various places around the world. People like Ayatollah Khomeini and Osama bin Laden demonstrate that persons with a religious fervor can and do impact the political process. The ulama remained an important influence in political decisions until the twentieth century, when many Muslim countries adopted Western styles of government.

The impact of these developments resulted in diverse understandings of Islamic law and practice. The beliefs of the various legal schools were similar, but the Islamic standards for living could differ widely from one community to the next depending on the predominant legal school. The different legal schools may vary on the exact time of an afternoon prayer, whether invalids could hire someone to go on the pilgrimage on their behalf, whether a woman of age could marry someone not approved by her father or other male guardian, and whether pregnancy could be used in court as proof of fornication. These are just a few areas in which the various legal schools may differ.

Institutionalization of Dominant Schools (950–1900). The dominance of the various legal schools and the increasing

---

[10] Ibid. (Shafii countries include southern Egypt, the Arabian Peninsula, East Africa, Indonesia, Malaysia with some followers in Palestine, Jordan, and Syria. Hanbali countries include Saudi Arabia, Qatar, and Oman.)

dependence of the Islamic community on the ulama led to a stagnation of Muslim Law and the closure of creative reasoning. During this long period of Islamic history, regional differences continued result in varying viewpoints. The focus of Islamic law at this time was to look for a precedent or *taqlid*.[11] The legal codes became far more detailed during these nine and one-half centuries. The role of the Hadith, non-Qur'anic traditions, began to significantly impact the interpretation of Islamic Law during this time period.

The Final Phase (1900-current). After a long period of institutionalization and stagnation, the westernization of the Muslim countries brought fresh winds of change related to Islamic law. The focus moved away from the dominance of the ulama and from legal precedents. Instead, the emphasis was original thinking in hope that Islamic law would emerge from its stagnancy. The Shi'ites were those who insisted that original thinking or *ijtihad* was needed without one clear leader over all of Islam. They believed that those who were qualified to present these original thoughts or *mujtahid* would provide the necessary leadership in the absence of the visible Imam.[12] Islamic Modernists, who were often educated in the West, wanted to go beyond the tedious legal documents created by the traditional legal schools and focus on the Qur'an. The result was a legal perspective that attempted to wed dynamic Qur'anic principles with an industrialized world. Debate exists on whether the Islamic law instituted in Afghanistan and parts of Nigeria represent a step back to the fifth phase in Islamic history (the institutionalization of dominant schools) or the creation of a hybrid legal perspective that selectively chooses

---

[11] Ibid.
[12] Ibid., 116.

which texts and how to use them in a world considered hostile to the kind of community established by Muhammad in Medina.

Five Categories of Muslim Laws

Mandatory Laws. As noted in chapter 3, one of the laws that became binding, or mandatory, for all Muslims was praying five times a day, a law revealed to Muhammad prior to his move to Medina during his mystical journey into the various levels of heaven. When the Muslim community lived in Mecca, they offered prayers in the direction of Jerusalem, but in Medina they turned toward Mecca. Muhammad made the change of direction during one period of prayer, and the community followed his example. Also in Medina, the five prayers each day became mandatory for all Muslims, but not for the Jews who lived there. One can see that the requirement to pray five times each day comes from the Qur'an (11:114), but the requirement to pray in the direction of Mecca came from the action of Muhammad. From that time, all Muslims are required to pray five times each day in the direction of Mecca. Later qualifiers were added to the daily prayers, including the Shi'ite addition of the phrase "Ali is the friend of Allah," the exact time each prayer should be performed in a particular region, whether "amen" can be said after reciting the first chapter of the Qur'an, and others.

A second mandatory practice, as noted in chapter 3, established in Medina was the almsgiving or zakat tax to care for the widows and orphans. The amount as alms was calculated on the amount and type of wealth of the individual. Although the Qur'an mentions the collection of the mandatory tax several times, the specifics on how much tax based upon one's property came from the actions of the prophet Muhammad. Often 2 1/2 percent is the most common percentage, but the intent is for the wealthiest in society to help bear the burdens of those who cannot fend for themselves. The zakat remains mandatory for all Muslims. Debate exists today on how the money collected through the zakat should be used, whether only to assist the destitute in the community or to fund the nation's military.

A third mandatory practice instituted by Muhammad was the observance of the fast during the month of Ramadan as first discussed in chapter 3. Established in the Qur'an 2:184–188), the fast became a requirement of all Muslims. The ill or those experiencing traveling fatigue can be exempt, but they should make up the fast at a future time (2:184). Exemption is also provided to those who cannot fast without severe hardship (2:184). Muslims would eventually recognize that the temporary exemption could also extend to one serving in the military and women who recently gave birth and that those under hardship, such as the very young and the very old, did not have fast or make it up at a later time. Many of the qualifications of those who were temporarily or outright exempt from the fast were developed by the legal schools long after the death of Muhammad.

A fourth mandatory practice in Muhammad's day was the pilgrimage to Mecca. The second chapter of the Qur'an (verses 196–203) establishes the importance of fulfilling the pilgrimage to Mecca. About two million Muslims make this journey each year during the month of Hajj. Some legal schools allow for an invalid to pay for someone to go on the pilgrimage to Mecca on their behalf because they are physically unable to fulfill the requirements of the pilgrimage. A more detailed description is provided in chapter 3.

The four examples above are mandatory for each Muslim, but other laws are obligatory for the community. These laws include the conducting of prayers at a Muslim funeral and coming together for the Friday Prayer Service. In addition to the mandatory laws, other laws were created and strongly recommended, but not required of all Muslims.

One other mandatory practice during the days of Muhammad and the early Muslim community was the tax for non-Muslims living in a portion of the Islamic Empire. Those persons who were monotheists (Jews, Christians, and Zoroastrians) were called *dhimmi* and allowed to live among the Muslims as long as they did not attempt to convert Muslims to their religion. The *dhimmi* were required to pay a poll tax called *jizya* which provided for their protection by the Muslim army. The *dhimmi* were not allowed to serve in the military, but they were granted protection by the Muslim army in exchange for this required tax that helped to support the Muslim military.

Recommended Behavior. As in most ethical and/or legal systerm one can find both mandatory and recommended actions. The zakat tax is required of all Muslims, while *sadaqat* (almsgiving) is recommended but not required. Muslims are encouraged to give to charities and to individuals who are lacking in financial resources, but this is viewed as a voluntary act that goes beyond the required zakat tax.

In the same way, praying five times a day is mandatory for all Muslims, while praying at night after the last of the required prayers is recommended but not required. Another recommended behavior is to offer supplemental prayers similar to the five daily prayers.

The fast during the month of Ramadan is required of all Muslims, but Muslims are also encouraged to fast during the months of Rajab and Sha'ban. Fasting during these months is not intended to replace the fast during Ramadan, but it is encouraged as an act of piety. Muslims are encouraged to eat in the morning before the fast begins, but this is not required. During the Iraq War, many Muslims called for a pause in the military activity during the month of Ramadan due to a recommendation tracing back to the life of Muhammad. Debate among Muslims ensued over whether fighting should take place during the month of Ramadan.

Other recommended behaviors for Muslims include greeting one another, visiting with friends and neighbors, and showing hospitality to strangers. For some Muslims, circumcision is considered mandatory, but for others it is a recommendation rather than a requirement.

Disapproved Behavior. Just as some actions are recommended but not required in Islamic law, there are actions that are discouraged but not forbidden. Discouraged actions include sleeping after sunrise, false advertising, seeking revenge, boasting about oneself, lying, and making fun of others. Behavior that does not violate mandatory laws but goes against the spirit of the law would be deemed an undesirable or disapproved behavior.[13]

Permissible Behavior. When a behavior is not required or forbidden, recommended or discouraged, then it is considered permissible. Islamic law neither approves nor disapproves of

---

[13] See http://www.shirazi.org.uk/makruh.htm for more disapproved behaviors listed by a Shi'ite source.

such behaviors. Polygamy, with a limit of four wives, is permitted in Islamic law. During the time of the fast, in the month of Ramadan, breaking the fast is permissible if a woman is in the final stage of pregnancy, nursing a child, or going through menstruation. Other allowed reasons for breaking the fast include illness, a heavy travel schedule, old age, and being a child not yet old enough to fast. Smoking tobacco is a permissible and common behavior in many Muslim countries.

Forbidden Behavior. Islamic law recognizes many actions as taboo or forbidden. Muslim law does not allow a Muslim to be an atheist or to associate anyone or anything as equal to God. Failing to submit faithfully to the required laws of Islam, such as the daily prayers, the fast, almsgiving, etc., is forbidden. Muslims are forbidden to desecrate a holy place such as a mosque. Also forbidden is improper touching between a man and a woman who are not married. Most Muslims consider adultery, sodomy, and homosexuality forbidden. Gambling, dancing, accepting false teachings, converting to another religion, and bearing false testimony are generally considered forbidden actions.[14]

Dietary Laws provide another set of taboos that identify the food and drink that is unacceptable for the Muslim to ingest.[15] Muslims are not to eat food that died or was killed in an improper way, meaning animals must be killed by cutting the jugular vein and then the blood must be drained. Islamic dietary laws are very similar to those of Judaism. Both groups forbid pork and any animal that feeds on other animals.

---

[14] See http://www.shirazi.org.uk/haram.htm for more forbidden behaviors listed by a Shi'ite source.

[15] See Surah 2:172; 5:4; 16:115.

Muslims are allowed to eat creatures from the sea which are forbidden in Judaism, but Muslims are not allowed to drink wine which is allowed in Judaism.[16] Also eating meat that has been sacrificed or dedicated to a deity other than Allah is forbidden.[17]

A few other interesting actions that are forbidden, according to Yusuf al-Qaradawi include: taking mind altering drugs, men wearing gold and silk ornaments, having statues of any kind, having dogs as indoor pets, serving in a military that is fighting with Muslims, fornication and adultery.[18]

Conclusion

The lists above may provide the reader with a mistaken notion that all actions clearly fit into one of the five categories. Because several different legal schools exist, varying interpretations also exist. What one Muslim community requires may simply be recommended or permissible in another community. Veiling is an example of an action understood differently in various parts of the Muslim world. Some places require that a woman wear a veil in public, while others recommend the behavior or simply consider the practice to be permissible. Also, the penalty for breaking a law may differ from place to place. A Muslim found guilty of theft may be imprisoned in one country, but in Saudi Arabia his hand may be amputated. A person found guilty of adultery may be imprisoned, beaten, or even stoned to death depending on where the offense is tried.

---

[16] Wine is forbidden in Surahs 2:119 and 5:93.

[17] Surah 6:119, 121.

[18] Yusuf al-Qaradawi, *Al-Halal Wal Haram Fil Islam (The Lawful and the Prohibited in Islam)*, Kamal El-Helbawy et al. Eds., Plainfield, IN: American Trust Publications, 1994.

Although the categories are clear, the interpretation of what belongs in each category often differs from one Muslim country to another. The penalty for breaking such laws may also differ greatly. Muslims who live in a secular country such as the United States or Great Britain will only be tried for crimes recognized by the state; therefore, adultery and atheism, while forbidden in Islamic law, are not crimes for which a court will try them. One exception to this is the existence of a sharia arbitration court in Ontario, Canada, that can be used to ease the backlog of cases in the Ontario judicial system. Muslims may choose this option, but they are not required to do so.

One must understand the legal school that is the authority for a particular country or c ommunity to understand how the laws are classified and what punishment follows conviction of particular offenses. One other concept that is essential to understanding Islamic law in the twenty-first century is *fatwa*. A *fatwa* is a legal opinion offered by a qualified person trained in Islamic law to clarify the correct interpretation of a particular law. Persons like Osama bin Laden have used *fatwas* to provide guidance to Muslims on how to live in the world today. Such legal opinions are only binding on those who recognize the qualifications of the individuals issuing the *fatwas*.

Chapter 7

a picture of
islam and modernity

To understand the challenges facing contemporary Islam, one must first explore a major shift that drastically changed the world and especially Europe and North America. Sociologists call the change "modernity." In short, a massive change took place in the nineteenth century that radically reshaped the social, economic, and philosophical foundations of Europe and North America. These changes moved the Western world from the medieval period into the so-called modern period. A series of revolutions impacted people's worldview and ultimately the world itself.

Many of the readers of this manuscript may wonder why so much attention should be paid to modernity when post-modernism is the rage. In reality, Americans and Europeans are experiencing a shift away from the impact of modernity to another paradigm that is still taking shape. The reader must realize that much of the world is still struggling with the impact of modernity as they address changes related to urbanization and industrialization that have been part of American and European life for more than 200 years.

One revolution took place in the area of scientific inquiry. A series of scientific discoveries such as the earth rotating around the sun, the existence of additional planets, gravity, etc.

gave scientists the optimism that science could explain anything of relevance. The center of scientific understanding moved from the authority of the church to the authority of the scientific method. The optimism of science expanded to create theories of how human beings and the world came into existence that did not involve the Bible or the church as a source of authority. The result of this mental shift was the development of a materialistic view of the world and the stance that all of life's important questions could be both understood and mastered through the laboratory. The necessity of having faith in God gave way to having faith in the scientific method. Discovery and technology would lead to the scientific promised land, a secular society.

As a result of technological developments, products and information formerly limited to scholars became available to the masses. The printing press made literature available to large numbers of individuals, and people's educational level began to grow. The development of factories that could mass-produce products lowered prices and allowed greater access to the products. In order to run these factories, workers were needed. Thus, people who lived in rural areas began to move close to the factories to provide the labor. In order to bring workers to the factory, cities were built to provide housing, schools, hospitals, and other necessities for the work force.

The birth of factories gave rise to the modern planned city. Rural communities began moving en masse to these cities in hopes of a better life. Because individuals came from different homogeneous rural communities, the cities also created a heterogeneous community in which many rural traditions gave way to create an urban culture. Agricultural production faded in favor of industrial production. The workday became fixed, and lives changed accordingly. Arguably, the eating of three meals a day is a result of the industrial revolution.

The Protestant Reformation led to the development of many different Christian denominations. Yet one could never imagine the revolution that followed, which created an emphasis on individualism that became part of the core of modern Western society. Family occupations once passed down from generation to generation gave way to individuals choosing the path that matched their own skills and interests. The individuality of choosing one's occupation impacted the political atmosphere as kingdoms became nations.

In North America and Europe, life changed drastically during the 1800s. Individualism, industrialization, and urbanization drove individuals to take charge of their own lives as they attempted to create a better life for themselves and their children. They moved from areas where their families had been for generations, and as a result geographical mobility became the norm. Many outside of Europe and North America observed these developments, which led to an increase of immigration to these lands of opportunity.

While these major changes were taking place in Europe and North America, the Ottoman Empire was quickly collapsing and many Muslim areas came under the control of one or more European powers. The colonizing countries built cities in these countries, but unlike the European cities, they established resources primarily for the Europeans and not for the remainder of the population. The primary purpose of these cities was to provide a venue where the natural resources of that land could be gathered and sent back to Europe. The result was that few Africans, Asians, and others were able to benefit from the urban developments. This also created resentment among the indigenous persons against the Europeans.

During the twentieth century, Muslim countries around the world began to win independence from the Europeans, which provided them an opportunity to create a twentieth-century Islamic state. They had the opportunity to establish their own government and to create a social, economic, political, and religious environment that would be both modern and Islamic. The difficulty for countries like Pakistan, Bangladesh, Indonesia, Kenya, and others was in trying to blend Islam and modernity. Should they return to their way of life prior to the coming of the Europeans, or should they attempt to create a new world that merged their traditional way of life with the production-oriented European system? This dilemma continues to impact the non-Western world and particularly the Islamic world.

Islam and Modernity

To explore the reaction of Muslims around the world to the impact of modernity, we must first realize that all individuals respond differently to such changes. Some embrace modernity as a messiah, while others view it as a demon that should be exorcized. Sociologist John Wilson identified five different reactions to modernity that aid an understanding of the various ways Muslims around the world approach advances. As one explores these five categories or descriptions of Muslims, one may discover that these same categories can easily apply to Christianity, Judaism, Hinduism, and other religions.[1]

Secularists

One response to modernity is to embrace it and embody all for which it stands. Many of the early national Muslim leaders were educated in Europe, where they learned the principles they would use to govern in their homelands. They knew they had resources, and they could see from the economic developments in Europe and North America that economic power translates into political power. Muslim Secularists attempted to create nations in the image of the two most powerful socioeconomic models of the twentieth century, the capitalist system of the West or the communist system of the East.

In principle, the capitalism of Europe and North America allowed for religious freedom, whereas the communism of the Soviet Union viewed religion as a crutch needed by the weak. Yet, communism proved to be a popular choice for many Muslim countries because it allowed leaders to establish a strong administrative center that maintained both the stability of the state and the conformity of the community. Many Muslims considered the individual freedom of Western nations a possible threat to the unity of their communities.

From the beginning of Islam, one of the most important characteristics of the movement was unity, from the tribal unity of pre-Islamic Arabia to the unity of the Muslim community. Unity was maintained during the Caliphal empires, at least in theory. Communism provided a pretext for

---

[1] See John F. Wilson, "Modernity," in vol. 9 of *Encyclopedia of Religion*, ed. Mircea Eliade (New York: Macmillan Publishing Company, 1987) 21.

a strong unified community that would appease the religious principles of Islam but utilized a socioeconomic structure that allowed them to compete in a global market. The Ba'th Party came into being as a socialist party in Syria, and Saddam Hussein belonged to this party in Iraq. Others opted for the route of capitalism and sought to create a democratic, capitalistic society. Turkey was the first Muslim country to establish a Western government through the influence of Mustafa Kamal Ataturk. Still other nations, such as Jordan and Saudi Arabia, established kingdoms that allowed for a ruling family in a fashion similar to that of the Umayyads. Even in the kingdoms, the Muslims sought to develop their resources and compete on the world's economic stage.

Many Muslim leaders embraced modernity and tried to help their countries catch up with the industrial, technological, and economic developments of Europe and North America. They created banks that charged interest for loans and paid interest to investors. They created modern factories to gather their resources and market them to the world. Although these Muslim leaders were steadfast in bringing the Muslim nations into the twentieth century, not all Muslims shared their enthusiasm for incorporating modernity.

Modernists

One group that expressed concern about "buying into" capitalism or communism blindly could be called the Modernists. The Modernists were concerned about the socioeconomic development of their countries, but they were equally passionate about their religious identity. Their concern was that Muslim countries would become secular, with religion a secondary or private matter. Many Modernists also trained in

Europe and North America or received a Western style education in their own country. They believed they could begin with the religious ideals of Islam and use them to create a state that was both modern and Islamic. Modernists tried to find harmony between the principles of Islam and those found in the West. They supported the introduction of modern banks and factories, but they felt the need to show how these advancements did not conflict with Islam. They longed for a Muslim state that would flesh out the ideals of Islam, represent the best of modernity, and not embrace the cultural implications of a materialistic society.

The Modernists sought guidance directly from the Qur'an and not from the various traditions or Hadith. Using the principles they found in the Qur'an, Modernists argued for the equal treatment of men and women, the need for modern banks and factories, and the need for a Western style of education. A more in-depth presentation of the Modernist attempts to bridge Islam and modernity is addressed in chapter 8.

Traditionalists

While the Secularists and Modernists attempted to bring Muslim nations into the twentieth century, the Traditionalists found their hope in the past. They held dear the Qur'an and the Muslim traditions that had been passed down for generations. Instead of creating a "so-called" modern state, they desired to return to the life they had before the Europeans came upon their soil. They considered the impact of a secular state to be far too great on the praxis of Islam. While the nation created national courts and institutions, the Traditionalists reaffirmed their own local courts and institutions that would function as they did during the time of the great Muslim empires. While the nation changed, local communities served as a place where life would go on as it had for centuries.

The Traditionalists placed their faith in God as articulated through their religious leadership. Whether Sunni or Shi'ite, traditional Muslims believed they were entrusted with a legacy that began with the prophets of old then was reestablished by Muhammad and fleshed out through the Muslim traditions or Hadith. For these people the nation's leaders could write and rewrite constitutions, but their daily lives would reflect the values that were good enough for their parents and grandparents. Traditionalists did not share the passion of the Secularists or Modernists for a "modern" state. They viewed their Islamic beliefs and traditions as a treasure that must be maintained and taught to the next generation. They would remain a constant reminder to their leaders of their Muslim heritage as they sought to shape and reshape their country into a modern state that could compete on a global stage. Considering themselves the guardians of the Muslim story, they would continue to live out the story individually and in their local communities.

Revivalists

Another group that did not share the vision of the secular and Modernist Muslims can be referred to as the Revivalists. Some use the term "fundamentalist" to refer to these Muslims, but because it has a distinctive meaning arising out of the Christian tradition, I have chosen the word "Revivalist." The Revivalists share the concern of the Traditionalists that a wholesale adaptation or moderate adaptations of European ways and lifestyles will relegate Islam to a small segment of Muslim life.

Unlike the Traditionalists, they believe that changes must be made to establish the kind of Muslim communities that existed in the early days of Islam. Ironically, the Revivalists and the Modernists agree that reforms must be made to Islam in modern times; however, they do not agree on the methods necessary to accomplish this end.

The Revivalists distrust most things that come from the West. They believe that Muslims are in danger of losing the essence of their identity by adapting Western social, political, and economic principles. Adopting the principle is by implication adopting the culture, which brings unhealthy and un-Islamic elements into the community that could damage future generations. For Revivalists, the solution to the ills of Islam is not adopting Western structures and institutions, but rediscovering the institutions believed to be part of the earliest Muslim community. Whereas Modernists look forward to the future to seek solutions, Revivalists look to the past. They function from an ideology that attempts to model the earliest traditions of the Muslim community in Medina.

The difficulty faced by the Revivalists is that they eschew Western forms of education, which leaves them with a Traditionalist form of education. Yet they neither accept all the traditions of the Traditionalists nor reject all of the traditions of the West. The end result is that Revivalist Muslims have a tendency to be self-educated and appear to choose the traditions they will use while discarding those that seem to run contrary to their concept of the Muslim community. One can read the works of Revivalist writers like al-Banna or Mawdudi and see them coming to similar conclusions, but they use different roads to arrive at the common destination. Modernists have often criticized Revivalists for attempting to create a Muslim world that never existed except in the minds of the Revivalists themselves.

Revivalists can often motivate populations by selecting key Qur'anic texts and Islamic traditions in order to support their cause and plan of action. For example, Revivalists use Qur'anic texts that speak harsh words about the Meccan polytheists and suggest that the West is the intended subject of that Qur'anic text. They are masters of propaganda, igniting the emotions of people by finding a common enemy to their Islamic way of life. Early Revivalists targeted other Muslims to pressure them to conform to the Revivalist way of life, but more recently Western nations have been the target for pressure. The Revivalist argument suggests that the West is immoral and will always ally with the enemy of Islamic nations around the world, namely Israel. They refer to the military activities of the United States and Europe as an attack on Islam rather than an attack on terrorism. They also use loaded language with words like "crusades" to invoke the image of days gone by when Muslims perceived that Christian Europe attempted destroy Islam. Their aggressive stance makes it difficult for other Muslims to oppose them without being labeled as puppets of the West. The perspective of the Revivalists will be discussed further in the next chapter.[2]

New Religious Movements

One last classification of Muslims holds to ideas or practices that are not acceptable to either the Sunni or Shi'ite traditions. Many Muslims may question whether these groups represent

---

[2] Donald L. Berry, *Islam and Modernity through the Writings of the Islamic Modernist Fazlur Rahman*, vol. 1 of Islamic Studies (Lewiston NY: Edwin Mellen Press, 2003) 12–38.

true Islam. These religious movements identify themselves with Islam, but they have integrated non-Islamic elements as part of their beliefs and practices. This response to modernity recognizes that God's revelation continued through individuals long after the death of Muhammad. Typically, these groups also have writings, in addition to the Qur'an, that carry the authority of scripture.

Bahai represents on example of a religious movement birthed in the context of Islam but whose beliefs stretched beyond the boundaries of orthodox Islam. Bahai shares the following common beliefs with Islam: one God exists and is referred to as Allah; God gives revelations to prophets, and the Qur'an is one of those revelations; the concept of mahdi or messiah is an important teaching of Islam; and missions are essential. Yet with all these commonalities, the differences between the two are significant.

The Bahai recognize that the door of prophecy did not end with the death of Muhammad; they believe the Bahullah was the promised mahdi or messiah. His writings have gained an importance comparable to scripture. In the latter part of the twentieth century, the list of prophetic figures recognized by the Bahai included names like Confucius and Krishna. They also recognize the scriptures of other religious traditions as valuable to their search for an understanding of God. They imply that just as the emergence of Islam superseded Christianity, Bahai superceded Islam. Although the Bahai embrace their roots in Islam, they also recognize that their spiritual inspiration also comes from the insights found in other religions.

A second group that represents this response to modernity is called the Nation of Islam. The Nation of Islam shares many important beliefs with orthodox Islam, such as the belief in one God whom they call Allah, the revelations of God through prophets, the divine judgment, the concept of the mahdi, and the importance of missions. The differences between the groups are important to note. The Nation of Islam believes that Elijah Muhammad was taught by Allah who came in human form in the person of W. D. Fard and treats his writings as scripture. Elijah Muhammad became the prophet of Allah, according to Nation of Islam, in spite of the Islamic teaching that Muhammad was the seal or last of the prophets. Savior's Day is celebrated each year to commemorate the life of W. D. Fard.

The greatest difference is that while Islam seeks to bring all persons together through its teachings and practices, the Nation of Islam holds that African Americans are to segregate themselves from European Americans. Malcolm X discovered the folly of this last principle when he went on pilgrimage to Mecca. When he returned from his journey, he began teaching orthodox Islam to the chagrin of the Nation of Islam.[3] Today, Louis Farrakhan leads the Nation of Islam.

These are only two of the groups that have appealed to sources outside the Qur'an and the Sunnah of Muhammad to deal with the stresses and challenges of modernity. Other older groups, such as the Druze Muslims in Lebanon and the Ahmadiyya in Pakistan and parts of West Africa, reflect groups that are not as well known in North America or Europe.

---

[3] See Gilles Kepel, *Allah in the West: Islamic Movements in America and Europe* (Palo Alto CA: Stanford University Press, 1997) 15–78.

Muslims in North America

Accounts differ on when the first Muslims arrived in North America. Some Muslim historians suggest that Muslims from Spain arrived as early as the tenth century, while others suggest that the first Muslims came from West Africa as early as 1312. Still other Muslim sources claim that the first Muslims arrived as African slaves in 1530. The first traceable theory points to the arrival of African Muslim slaves in the seventeenth to nineteenth centuries. During the collapse of the Ottoman Empire in the nineteenth and twentieth centuries, Muslims began to immigrate to the United States. Another source of Muslim immigration came through refugees from Iran, Lebanon, Bosnia, Albania, and Afghanistan during periods of revolution or conflict. In 1965, the United States changed its immigration policy from a quota system that favored European immigrants to a balanced immigration policy that opened the door for an increase in Muslims from all over the world.

One must recognize that a large disparity exists between Muslim and non-Muslim sources on the number of Muslims in North America. The following data comes from Bridges TV—American Muslim Lifestyle Network survey on American Muslim demographics.[4] According to the survey more than 1,200 mosques can be found in the United States, and more than half of them have been established since 1980. The current growth rate for Islam in the United States is 6 percent

---

[4] The data provided comes from the United States Census Bureau 2000; Zogby International, August 2000; Cornell University, April 2002; and "Mosque in America," a survey released in April 2002. The data can be obtained on the Allied Media Corporation web page: http://www.allied-media.com.

per year. Muslims in the United States are younger than the national average and more educated than the average American. Many Muslims came to this country for undergraduate or graduate study. The most common occupations for Muslims in America are student, engineer, physician/dentist, and homemaker. As many as 30 percent of Muslims in America are converts to Islam. About two million Muslims are associated with a local mosque in the United States, although the survey suggests that seven million Muslims live in the United States. The ethnicities of those associated with a mosque are South Asian (30 percent; India, Bangladesh, Pakistan, and Afghanistan), African American (30 percent), and Arab American (25 percent).[5]

All sources of information agree that Islam is growing in the United States through biological growth, immigration, and conversions. A significant place for Muslim conversions is in the prison system. The American Muslim Demographics Survey estimates that almost one-third of the African American converts to Islam come through Muslim prison ministries. The Muslims of North America probably represent all five categories listed earlier in the chapter. Most Muslims in the United States view the actions of al-Qa'eda (the agency of Osama bin Laden) as acts of terrorism rather than a justifiable defense of Islam against Western aggression.

I would estimate that a minority group in the United States support the agenda of Osama bin Laden, while a larger group understands his motives but disagrees with his methods. I would suggest that most Muslims in the United States are

---

[5] The other 15% includes Sub-Saharan African, European, White American, Southeast Asian, Caribbean, Turkish, Iranian, Hispanic/ Latino.

ashamed of the image of Islam portrayed by Osama bin Laden. I do not have statistical data to support these opinions, but I do believe that they reflect the situation in the United States in the early twenty-first century. The reader must remember that the attraction for many Muslims moving to the United States and Canada being able to live without the religious fanaticism found in some parts of the Muslim world. According to the Council on American-Islamic Relations Survey on American Muslim Voters, 82% said that terrorist attacks harm American Muslims, and, although this is important, 55% of those surveyed are afraid that the War on Terror has become a war on Islam. The results of this survey point to an American Muslim population that does not clearly support terrorism and fear that terrorism will eventually impact them negatively.[6]

---

[6]http://www.cair-net.org/pdf/american_muslim_voter_survey_2006.pdf.

Chapter 8

a picture of
contemporary Islam

As mentioned in chapter 7, colonization had a powerful impact on contemporary Islam. Although colonization flourished in the sixteenth century, the colonization of the nineteenth and twentieth centuries proved to have the greatest impact on the Islamic world. Countries like Great Britain, France, Spain, Russia, the Netherlands, Portugal, and Italy extended their influence to lands throughout the globe. Most Muslim countries came under the influence of one or more of these European powers. The ability of the Europeans (considered Christendom by many Muslims) to gain control of Muslim lands caused a crisis of faith for many Muslims around the world. Many of the Muslims believed that the political expansion of the various empires was due to their commitment to God and dedication to the teachings of Islam.

Once political power shifted to the Europeans, a religious crisis created the question as to why would Allah allow Muslim countries to fall under control of the West. Some Muslims attributed the loss of political power to the lack of technology, and for these persons, the Secularists and Modernists sought to help the Muslim community catch up on the technology that allowed the Europeans to gain a powerful position. Other Muslims believed that the defeat at the hands of the Europeans lay in the inadequacy of the Muslim community to fulfill the demands of the Islamic faith. For these persons, a great reform was necessary to rededicate all Muslims to the teachings of Islam. Many of the Revivalist movements emerged to encourage a stricter, more faithful observance of Islamic law. European colonization prepared the ground for both the secular and Modernist movements in Islam as well as the Revivalist movements, even though their solutions to the issues facing contemporary Islam differed dramatically.

Some of the early Revivalist movements emerged in non-colonized countries, but their influence would spread to impact Muslim countries throughout the globe. The Mahdi movement in Sudan, the Fulani movement in Nigeria, and the Padri movement in Sumatra are all examples of such movements, but the most influential proved to be the Wahhabi movement in Saudi Arabia. The Wahhabi movement could easily have disappeared from current history except for the fact that it provided the groundwork for the modern kingdom of Saudi Arabia. With the wealth produced by oil and its acceptance by the Saudi royal family, the influence of the movement gained notoriety among Muslims around the world.

Most of these movements drew from the writings of the medieval Muslim theologian Ibn Taymiyya, who advocated that the primary goal of human existence is not to know or study God or even to love God, as the Sufis argued, but to serve God through worship and obedience. He criticized harshly all unbelievers, including Muslims who were not being faithful to teachings of Islam, and he challenged Muslims to rededicate themselves to the Islamic ideals and faithful service to God. He and those who sought guidance through his teachings believed that the failure of Islam against the

Europeans was due to the Muslim lack of obedience to God and the causes of God.

The nineteenth century saw the emergence of the first Muslim Modernists who believed they could take the best of European technology and still remain faithful to the teachings of Islam. Somehow Islamic orthodoxy and European technology could partner so that Muslim nations could return as a political and economic force in the world without sacrificing the integrity of the faith. Men like Jamal al-Din al-Afghani of India and Muhammad Abduh of Egypt represent two of the important early Muslim Modernists. They advocated that the religious observances of Islam were universal, yet many of the social practices found in Muslim countries could be reformed to accommodate contemporary European societies. These two men and people like Sayyid Ahmad Khan suggested that Islam should take the best from the Europeans while being dedicated to the essentials of the religion. The result of this merger of ideas would be the establishment of independent Muslim countries that could compete on the political and economic world stage.

The Modernists and the Secularists combined to work toward creating independent Muslim countries, and when independence was won in the twentieth century they sought to implement their new visions for being both Muslim and modern. Nationalist movements dominated the independence movements rather than visions of a restored Caliphate that would be over Muslims throughout the world. As mentioned earlier, Saudi Arabia chose the ideology of the Wahhabi Revivalist movement as a guide to live out the Muslim life as an independent nation, whereas countries like Turkey chose to follow a secular, European model to live in a world dominated by Europe and North America. To proceed further, one must address some of the key theological, political, social, and economic issues Muslims face today in the twenty-first century.

Theological Issues

One key theological issue involves the sources for Islamic authority. All Muslims recognize that the Qur'an is God's revelation to the world given to Muhammad, yet Muslims differ on the use of the Qur'an. For some Muslims, certain passages have been abrogated or replaced by later revelations in the Qur'an that supersede them. Other Muslims suggest the whole of the Qur'an should be used without any verses being abrogated. The Revivalists and the Traditionalists usually accept the principle of abrogation, whereas the Modernists tend to point to the importance of all Qur'anic verses. Related to the issue of the Qur'an is the use of the written traditions of Islam, or the Hadith. Modernists tend to relegate most Hadith as historically questionable and therefore rely far more on the Qur'an than on Hadith material. Traditionalists and Revivalists usually draw heavily from the Hadith. Many of the promises made to Muslims who agree to take part in suicide bombings are based on Hadith material rather than the Qur'an. Another important assertion of many Modernists was that the term "Caliph" (khalipha) was not merely a political designation but a call of stewardship for all Muslims.

A second issue relates to the definition of what makes a good Muslim. Is orthodoxy, or right belief, more important than orthopraxy, right practice? Should correct beliefs be the determining factor in being a good Muslim, or should it be the faithful practice of Islamic law? In addition to the question of the primacy of orthodoxy or orthopraxy is whether Muslim communities can live with theological diversity or heterodoxy.

A third theological issue is related to Islam's proper relationship with Jews and Christians. Jews and Christians are esteemed in the early revelations of the Qur'an because they had received written revelations from God. However, in the later revelations of the Qur'an, the people of the book, as the Qur'an refers to them, receive harsh criticism. Because of their rejection of abrogation, the Modernists tend to believe that Jews and Christians believe in one God or are monotheists. Because of their acceptance of abrogation, the Traditionalists and Revivalists take a much harsher view of Jews and Christians. Some revisionists consider that neither Jews nor Christians are monotheists because the Jews associate the prophet Ezra with God and Christians associate the prophet Jesus with God.

A fourth important theological issue is whether morality can be legislated or must come from personal piety. Modernists and those identified with the Sufi movement tend to focus more on morality as an extension of personal piety. Fazlur Rahman, one of the best-known Muslim Modernists in Europe and North America in the twentieth century, suggested the source of morality was piety. The term *taqwa* is usually translated "piety," but Fazlur Rahman identified the term as an inner light or guide that was the source for morality. For the Revivalists and Traditionalists, morality relates directly to the obedience that must be mandated by the Muslim community. For this reason, these groups desire to mandate *shariah* or traditional Islamic law based on the Qur'an and the Sunnah of the prophet Muhammad. At stake is the question of whether morality must emerge from a pious life or be established by the passing of particular Islamic laws.

Although many other theological issues could be listed here, *jihad* is one of the most significant. The term *"jihad,"* as mentioned in chapter 3, literally means struggle. The modernists emphasize that the primary *jihad* is the personal struggle to combat one's lack of faith or obedience, and the lesser *jihad* is the struggle for the cause of God in one's community. Modernists often use *"jihad"* to refer to an educational, political, or social reform within their own country.

For the Revivalists, the term *"jihad"* has been used primarily for the war against all enemies of Islam. Since Europe and North America represent a distraction and deviate from Islam, the Europeans and North Americans are enemies to Islam, according to the Revivalists. Because Europeans and particularly Americans are all agents of the cultural traditions that landed on Muslim soil during colonization and continue to impact Muslim youth around the world through television, movies, and literature, Revivalists often do not distinguish between military and civilians. In one of his early public interviews, Osama bin Laden declared to the world that he did not distinguish between military and civilian targets in the war against Europeans and Americans. For the Revivalists, an attack on the World Trade Center or a United States embassy is an attack against the enemy who prevents Islam from regaining its rightful place in the world. A more in-depth discussion of the perspective held by the radical Revivalists can be found at the end of this chapter.

Political Issues

A host of political issues face Muslims today, but for the sake of brevity a few key issues are identified here to help readers understand the plight of Muslims in the twenty-first century. One issue relates to the form and authority held in a Muslim nation. What form of government is acceptable for a large or majority Muslim community? Today, one can find Muslim nations that are officially called republics, democratic republics, socialist republics, and kingdoms. Because of the unity perceived in the socialist political system, many Muslim countries chose that model such as the Ba'ath Party in Syria and Iraq. Lybia is one of the few Muslim countries that still has the word "socialist" as part of its official title. The most common title used by Muslim countries is republic or Islamic republic. In the republic, based on the Greek or Hellenistic model, leaders who are either appointed or elected by a popular vote represent the masses. Most Muslim countries today are republics that have elected or chosen leaders who create the laws that govern the land. One dilemma created by the republic is the question of who is qualified to represent the masses. Should it be a political or religious figure? In places like Iran, those considered trustworthy are leaders with high religious qualifications because of the Shi'ite teachings, whereas Sunni countries may seek the ulama or religious leadership in an advisory role or, in some cases, the political and religious role. Are political leaders trustworthy if they are not trained religious leaders? This question is currently up for debate in the Islamic world.

Another key issue is whether nationalism is a natural development of Islam or the Caliphate is the only natural or acceptable form of government. Several attempts were made in the twentieth century to restore a Caliphal system that would provide political stability and religious consistency throughout the Muslim world, yet the power of nationalist movements made such efforts all but impossible. The opponents of nationalism hold that having separate Muslim nations is a result of the corruption of Europe and the United States. These opponents believe that Muslims must be united through their religious and political structures to maintain the values of the earliest Muslim community. Modernists and Secularists hold that nationalism does not conflict with the values of Islam. The debate also exists as to whether a democratic method can be used to select national leaders. The Shi'ites believe the religious leaders are trustworthy and know what must be done to be faithful to Islam. The implication for the Shi'ites is that the masses are not capable of choosing their own leaders, and therefore a democratic election only opens the door for losing the religious and political edge that is Islam. Sunnis are more open to free elections because they used a similar election in choosing Abu Bakr as the first leader of the Muslim community following Muhammad's death. The choice was made not by popular vote, but rather by the vote of the trusted companions of the prophet Muhammad. This election or selection (*shura* or consultation) is the basis for supporting elections of leaders in Muslim countries today.

Another key political issue is the understanding and treatment of non-Muslims. Modernists and Secularists usually support religious freedom within a Muslim country. The foundation of religious freedom goes back to the days of Muhammad, who allowed other monotheists, Jews and Christians, to coexist with the Muslim community as long as they did not meet publicly or attempt to convert Muslims to their faith. Muhammad did not allow polytheists to continue living in Muslim lands, and he offered them the opportunity to convert or to do battle. The Traditionalists hold strictly to their understanding of Muhammad's methodology; therefore, they allow limited freedom of persons from other religious backgrounds. Because they may not accept the fact that Jews and Christians are monotheists, the Revivalists typically do not believe that Jews and Christians are monotheists and often consider all those who live in a Muslim state to be bound by Muslim law.

This issue not only relates to dealing with non-Muslims within the nation but also impacts the approach to the United Nations. Secularists and Modernists tend to work with the United Nations, whereas the Traditionalists and especially the Revivalists tend to see a relationship with the United Nations as acceptance of European and American ideals that conflict with the values of Islam.[1] Debate continues on what role Islam and Islamic law should play in the federal laws of these independent Muslim countries. The debate has led many countries to edit their constitutions due to pressures from both global political allies and from Muslims who demand that Islam be part of the fabric of their national identity and policies. These are just a few of the political issues facing contemporary Islam.

---

[1] Abdullahi Ahmed An-Na'im, *Toward an Islamic Reformation: Civil Liberties, Human Rights, and International Law* (Syracuse: Syracuse University Press, 1990) provides an excellent discussion of Islam and the efforts of the United Nations.

Social Issues

Once again, the number of social issues Muslims face today requires more space than is possible in this chapter, but some issues stand out as vitally important for uniting or dividing the Muslim community. Most Muslims recognize that the Qur'an provides guidance for the rights and responsibilities of each Muslim; however, not every Muslim agrees on the basic human rights. Some Muslims consider birth control a necessity for halting overpopulation in countries that cannot afford an unhindered increase in numbers, while others consider birth control to be paramount to playing God. Some Muslims would support abortion in the first trimester, consider in vitro fertilization as an acceptable way to conceive children, and allow for euthanasia in extreme circumstances; however, many Muslims consider all of these options as attempts to make choices that should be left to God.[2]

Those who differ on the issues cited above often debate whether the human rights declaration used by the United Nations should be binding on Muslims. In an effort to be compatible with the human rights standards of the United Nations, many Muslim countries have passed Muslim family laws that provide similar rights for women as would be found in Europe and the United States. Some local communities protest these laws by functioning under a more traditional set of Islamic laws that are governed by local Muslim courts. Great debate exists on the understanding of the rights and proper roles of men and women. Some areas keep the traditional

---

[2] See Fazlur Rahman, *Health and Medicine in the Islamic Tradition* (Chicago: Kazi Publications, 1998) for an excellent discussion of bio-ethical issues from a Muslim perspective.

stance that two women witnesses are equal to one male witness, but other Muslims suggest that men and women are equal in the eyes of God and should therefore have the same rights in Muslim society.

In regard to marriage and divorce, most Muslim countries have adapted their stances to be more in line with the marriage and divorce laws found in Europe and the United States. Traditionalists still emphasize arranged marriages that are contracted between the groom and a male member of the bride's family. They also suggest that the male must be the person to request a divorce. The practice of divorce by repudiation, with the male saying "I divorce you" three times, has been all but abolished in the Muslim world.

In most Muslim countries, marriages and divorces must be registered with the federal government. In many of these countries, women are permitted to initiate divorce proceedings. Polygamy or more specifically polyandry (multiple wives) is allowed in Islam with a limit of four. Traditional Islam also allowed an unlimited number of concubines or female slaves that were bought or taken captive. Today, few Muslim men have more than one wife. The Qur'an states that multiple wives are allowed "if you treat them equally" (4:3); Modernists usually suggest that this means the ideal is one man and one woman because it would be impossible to treat multiple spouses equally. Some suggest that the reason few Muslim men have multiple wives is because of the high cost of the bride price.

The bride price, which some might call a dowry, is the price paid by the groom in compensation for taking the bride from her family. The early principle held that the amount given was to be put aside for the bride should the groom not live up to the marriage contract, yet in many places the family receives the bride price as compensation for the loss of a family member and the bride no longer has access to the amount given. The latter practice can produce problems when a women is divorced and her family does not feel compelled to provide for her since she is no longer part of her birth family.

Throughout the world, Muslim Family Laws address other issues impacting women, such as inheritance laws, laws related to women testifying in court, and laws related to sexuality outside of marriage. Traditional Islamic law provides two-thirds of the inheritance to male children and one-third to female children. The logic behind this is that the females will receive compensation in the form of the bride price when they marry. Many Muslim Family Laws provide equal inheritance to both male and female children.[3] Grandchildren, who were not to receive an inheritance in traditional Islamic law, now receive a portion of the inheritance in some of the Muslim Family Laws. As mentioned earlier, traditional Islamic courts recognize that the testimony of two women is equivalent to the witness of one man, yet many of the Muslim Family Laws recognize the legitimacy of a witness regardless of gender.

Lastly, traditional Islamic law considers homosexuality, prostitution, premarital sex, or extramarital sex to be punishable offenses, whereas these are not always considered crimes in nontraditional Islamic courts. One can understand why Traditionalists and Revivalist have attempted to challenge

---

[3] Muslim Family Laws represent attempts by Pakistan and other countries to provide for women and children in a way that would be true to Islamic principles while in line with international human rights standards.

many of these laws: they view them as a corruption of Islam in an attempt to mirror the West.

Chapter 7 mentioned education as subject for debate. Muslims differ on the type of education that Muslim children and young adults should receive. Should Muslims receive a secular education in Europe or North America, study in a Western style school in their own country, or be educated in a traditional Muslim school? Another debate exists on the necessity or appropriateness of females receiving any form of education. During the reign of the Taliban in Afghanistan, female children were forbidden from attending school. In other settings, women can be educated only for certain professions. Many Muslim settings allow women to pursue a wide variety of careers, but the women often take care to dress modestly due to personal preference or to avoid drawing negative attention to themselves.

Economic Issues

Chapter 7 offered a brief discussion concerning the choice of communism or capitalism. These two economic systems were dominant during the time when most Muslim countries won their independence. The Modernists held that a person could combine the principles of one or both economic systems with Qur'anic principles to produce a dynamic model of contemporary Islam. Traditionalists and Revivalists insisted that these systems both promote economic values that are inconsistent with Islam. Although the approach of communism seemed popular for a time, most Muslim countries moved toward capitalism as the system of choice in the latter part of the twentieth century. The establishment of banks and other financial institutions created hope for Secularists but created a dilemma for Traditionalists and Revivalists. Traditionalist and Revivalists attempted to create alternative institutions that would function on time-honored Islamic traditions.

One debate that emerged in the banking community was the issue of interest. The Qur'an forbids the practice of *riba* or usury—lending or borrowing money with the intent of doubling or tripling the debt for use of the money (2:275–280). The debate flared on whether modern banking interest, based on supply and demand, was a form of riba. Secularists and Modernists concluded that modern banking interest was not the same as the forbidden practice of riba, whereas Traditionalists and Revivalists concluded that any form of banking interest was a violation of the Qur'an's teaching. The challenge for those who opposed modern banking interest was creating institutions that provide incentives for Muslim investors so they can somehow compete with their capitalistic counterparts who use interest to entice investors. Many nations have attempted to establish Islamic banks that do not pay interest for investors or charge interest for loans. One-time payments or charges attempted to replace the percentage interest offered or charged by Western-style banks. To this date, these Islamic banks have had difficulty surviving without subsidy from the federal or local government.

Another key economic issue is the interpretation and use of zakat. In chapter 3, zakat is identified as one of the pillars of Islam. Zakat was established as a tax that would care for the needs of widows and orphans in the Muslim community. Over time, the zakat tax produced more money, and its use expanded to include other important financial burdens of the Islamic Empire. Debate exists today as to whether zakat can only be used for relief work or also to support the military and the political structures necessary for maintaining the administration of the Islamic state. No debate exists on the necessity of collecting the zakat tax, but great debate exists on how the revenues are to be used in contemporary Islam.

Lastly, Muslim nations began to develop the economic resources to compete on the global economic stage, and the next challenge was to determine with whom they would partner without compromising their Islamic values. The question emerged, "Can a Muslim nation enter into an economic union with a nation or corporation that does not share the belief in God or share the values that are important to Islam?" With the discovery of abundant oil late in the twentieth century, the Muslim oil countries could choose to develop their own economic unions such as OPEC. The problem arose for the oil countries when they needed resources not available in Muslim lands, and the greater problem arose for non-oil countries because they did not have the bargaining power of the OPEC nations.

Debate exists on whether Muslims should develop economic unions to compete with Western unions or whether each nation should act in a manner that brings economic benefit to itself regardless of the beliefs and values of its economic partners. To this date, the latter approach seems dominant, as Muslim nations such as Indonesia and Malaysia have developed partnerships with Western-based corporations that produce tennis shoes, clothes, and other goods. Many brands of tennis shoes are made in Muslim countries in East or Southeast Asia, yet Traditionalists and Revivalists seek ways to develop economic partnerships with other Muslim countries that would ultimately benefit the Muslim world and lessen economic dependence on Europe and North America. These are but a few of the economic issues facing Muslim countries around the globe. Although oil has made the Gulf States some of the richest countries in the world, countries with large populations such as Sudan and Bangladesh are also some of the poorest of the world. The challenge of the economic development of nations remains in conflict with the economic development of Muslim countries.

Revolution or Reformation

The issues listed in this chapter represent a great divide on how the Muslim nation should look and function. Some Muslims believe governments and other institutions can be reformed, while others hold that the needed changes demand a revolutionary way of thinking to adhere to the values and traditions of Islam.

The history of Islam is filled with groups who attempted either to rebel against the rulers of the community or sought to make important changes for the sake of the community. One of the earliest rebel groups emerged during the Caliphate of Ali. In chapter 5, the reader was introduced to a group of rebel soldiers called the Kharijites who felt betrayed by Ali's willingness to negotiate with Mu'awiya. They took to arms to combat Ali and his army, and, although they were defeated in battle, a member of the group succeeded in assassinating Ali. The rebellious spirit of this group continued during the Umayyad and Abbasid empires. They represent the spirit of revolution that has reemerged at different times in Muslim history. The Kharijites developed an ideology that focused on the outward expressions of Islam. When a Caliph failed to follow the guidance of Allah, the Kharijites were obliged to remove that person from office so that a more faithful Muslim leader could fill the role.[4]

A second group that strived to make changes in Islam was the Sufis. They sought to reform Islam by reemphasizing the spiritual elements because they felt that legalism had relegated Islam to a system of laws without the dynamic spiritual strength of the early Muslims. Sufis did not resort to military activity to accomplish their goals, but rather sought to restore the spiritual dynamics of the early community one Muslim at a time. Their orders provided a context for spiritual development that would serve as a leaven so that Islam would rise to its full potential. Over time, Sufism became obsessed with spiritual encounters with God and lost track with the larger Muslim community. This eventually led to periods of great persecution. The reformer al-Ghazali sought Sufi ideals to bring reform to Islam. The emphasis on personal piety over legal codes resulted in the Sufis being perceived as a threat to the entirety of the Islamic Law or Shariah.[5]

A third group that attempted to make changes in the Islamic community was the Wahhabis. The Wahhabi movement, established in Saudi Arabia, desired to reemphasize the spiritual dynamics that were so important to the Sufis, but they began to use some of the techniques of the Kharijites. They looked to the writings of Ibn Taymiyya, who sought to bridge Islamic orthodoxy and orthopraxy. The Wahhabis tended to use Ibn Taymiyya's thoughts to justify a revival of Islamic law through political change, while ignoring the fact that Ibn

---

[4] H. A. R. Gibb and J. H. Kramers, *Shorter Encyclopedia of Islam* (Ithaca NY: Cornell University Press, 1965) 246–49.

[5] Fazlur Rahman, *Islam*, 2nd ed. (Chicago: University of Chicago Press, 1979) 146–47.

Taymiyya did not support the questioning of political leaders. Although they viewed themselves as a reform movement, they used an ideology and methodology similar to that of the Kharijites. The Wahhabi movement focused on condemning all the traditions and practices found in Saudi Arabia that they considered heretical. They, like the Kharijites, focused on the outward behavior of Muslims rather than their pietistic motivations for living the life of a Muslim. Any attempt to appeal to Muhammad or any other pious Muslim as an intercessor of Muhammad was condemned as heretical. The Wahhabis condemned pilgrimages to the tombs of pious Muslims in order to seek favor from them because this act implied intercession. These and other similar customs were not merely considered unhealthy; they were considered deeds of unbelief. The Wahhabi movement did not immediately impact Saudi Arabia when it first appeared in the eighteenth century, but the twentieth century provided fertile ground for its revival in Saudi Arabia.

Today, student associations, educational institutions, and missionary efforts all reflect the desire of Wahhabis to spread their ideology of religious conservativism and their methodology of taking a harsh line against all forms of perceived or potential heresy. One can see the impact of the Wahhabi efforts in the libraries of Muslim centers in various parts of the United States and in Great Britain. Not all Revivalist groups are to be traced to the Wahhabis, but those who espouse Wahhabi ideals today have impacted many Revivalist groups directly or indirectly.[6]

---

[6] For a brief history and critic of Wahhabism, see Hamid Algar, *Wahhabism: A Critical Essay* (Oneonta NY: Islamic Publications International, 2002).

The twentieth century saw not only the renewal of the Wahhabi movement, but the creation of several Revivalist movements that use many of the same sources as the Wahhabis. The Muslim Brotherhood in Egypt and the Jama'at-i-Islami from Pakistan represent movements that not only wish to change the internal direction of the Muslim community, but also see themselves as battling the impact of Western colonization. They sought to create alternative schools to compete with the increasing number of western-style schools in the Middle East and in South Asia. Although no direct link ties the Wahhabi movement and groups like the Jama'at-i-Islami to Osama Bin Laden, some Muslim and non-Muslim sources believe that Osama bin Laden sought refuge with members of the Jama'at-i-Islami when he had to flee Afghanistan. The middle of the twentieth century introduced many similar Revivalist groups. These groups typically were not created to have a universal appeal, but they focused on their own religious, political, and social contexts.

The end of the twentieth century provided a new chapter for the Revivalist efforts of Muslims around the world. One event that created a great rift between Muslims and the West was the establishment of the modern state of Israel. Muslims and Jews share a similar linguistic, cultural, and genetic heritage as discussed in chapter 1. At times Jews and Muslims have coexisted in peace, but the movement of Jewish settlers into what the Arabs called Palestine seemed to challenge the authenticity and traditions of Islam. Almost 900 years had passed from the time of the First Crusade until the modern state of Israel came into existence, but for many Arabs the appearance of Jewish crowds in the lands where they fought Crusaders opened a deep wound. The support of Great Britain and the United States for the modern state of Israel was and is taken as a slap in the face of Arab Muslims and Muslims around the world. To understand this perspective, one must read the words of an Arab reflecting on these thoughts:

> Today, on the eve of the third millennium, the political and religious leaders of the Arab world constantly refer to Saladin (a famous general who fought the Crusaders), to the fall of Jerusalem and its recapture. In the popular mind, and in some official discourse, too, Israel is regarded as the new Crusader state.... The Arabs perceived the Suez expedition of 1956 as a Crusade by the French and the English, similar to that of 1191....
>
> In a Muslim world under constant attack, it is impossible to prevent the emergence of a sense of persecution, which among certain fanatics takes the form of a dangerous obsession. The Turk Mehmet Ali Agea, who tried to shoot the pope on 13 May 1981, had expressed himself in a letter in these terms: "I have decided to kill John Paul II, supreme commander of the Crusades." Beyond this individual act, it seems clear that the Arab East still sees the West as a natural enemy. Against that enemy, any hostile action—be it political, military, or based on oil—is considered no more than legitimate vengeance. And there can be no doubt that the schism between these two worlds dates from the Crusades, deeply felt by the Arabs, even today, as an act of rape.[7]

---

[7] Amin Maalouf, *The Crusades Through Arab Eyes*, trans. Jon Rothschild (London: Al Saqi Books, 1984) 265–66.

These thoughts reflect a proud people who view the involvement of Jewish and Christian nations in a land that they consider holy. Actions against Palestinians and other Muslims by Western armies is perennial and seen by many Muslims as a continuation of the Crusades.

Some of the political parties found in the Middle East and in other parts of the Muslim world have embraced the notion that America and its allies are continuing the Crusades in Afghanistan and Iraq. This attitude magnified during the first Gulf War, the invasion of Afghanistan, and the invasion of Iraq. People like Osama bin Laden have used the rhetoric of the Crusades to recruit and motivate Muslims to fight in the newest Crusade against the Arabs. Bin Laden was particularly upset when American troops were allowed to use Saudi Arabia as a staging area to combat the Iraqi army in defense of Kuwait. People like bin Ladin view any military presence of American or European troops as an invasion rather than a necessity for ending terrorist activities. The presence of Western movies, dress, institutions, and troops in the Muslim world is perceived as an attack on Islam. Thus, Revivalist groups have taken to the methods of the Kharijites, using military force to target key areas and expel all Western influence from their land. Since both civilians and soldiers carry this Western influence, Muslim radical groups make no distinction between military and civilian targets. Whether the target is the Two Towers or the London Subway system, the goal is the same: to remove all Westerners from Muslim lands and restore the glory of Islam.[8]

---

[8] For an in-depth overview of Revivalist movements throughout the history of Islam, see Fazlur Rahman, *Revival and Reform in Islam: A Study*

Summary

One can see that many important theological, political, social, and economic issues have created a sense of tension within Muslim countries and the larger Muslim world. Loyalty to the nation, which is primary loyalty to some, competes with loyalty to the larger Muslim community. These issues have created serious and passionate debates among the religious and political leadership of Muslim countries throughout the world. The approach to these issues by individual Muslims and Muslim groups influences how they interact with non-Muslim nations and groups politically and economically. For some the key issue is national survival, while the issue for others is the reestablishment of a unified Muslim community that is theologically, politically, socially, and economically united.

---

of Islamic Fundamentalism, ed. Ebrahim Moosa (Oxford: Oneworld Publications, 2000).

Chapter 9

A PICTURE OF
ISLAM IN PRAXIS

In most cultures around the world, important events in the life of each member of society are marked in some way. The birth of a child, a coming of age, marriage, and death, are often recognized with rituals and ceremonies by families and communities around the world. These events serve as important markers in the life cycle of the individual, but the rituals associated with these events are for the entire community to recognize their significance. Although the ceremonies may differ to some degree from one Muslim culture to another, Islam does recognize these events as important both to the individual and to the community at large.

Islamic Life Cycle

Most Muslims embrace the extended family. The extended family means uncles, aunts, cousins, nephews, and nieces are all considered an integral part of the family. For those raised in the rural southeastern United States, the idea of the extended family is familiar. In my own family, I use the terms "uncle" and "aunt" to refer to the cousins of my parents. In such a society, a family gathering or reunion can be a large affair. When the important events in the life of every Muslim are acknowledged, the whole community participates because of the importance of the extended family and community.

From the earliest teachings of Islam, having children is viewed as a blessing from God. Muslims are encouraged to marry and have children. Although Muhammad forbade the infanticide of female children practiced in pre-Islamic Arabia, the birth of a son is considered a special blessing for many Muslims today. When a child is born, the family and the whole community celebrate the new life. From day one, children are exposed to the call to prayer that they will hear five times each day for the rest of their lives. They often hear the first chapter of the Qur'an recited to them or the Surah al-Fatihah. Gifts are brought to honor a new child, and the community recognizes that God has provided this life to strengthen and preserve the family for the future. In many Muslim communities, sacrifices are made on the seventh day of life, and the child receives a name that may honor a respected relative or honor one of the heroes of the faith. The rituals resemble those in Judaism, except in Judaism the naming takes place on the eighth day and includes a circumcision of male children.

From birth until they come of age, children play together and are not usually restricted on the type of dress worn. However, when males or females come of age at twelve or thirteen, the expectations change for male and female behavior. During these adolescent years they are taught to memorize portions of the Qur'an in Arabic, even though many Muslim children do not speak Arabic. To mark the movement into puberty, male children are circumcised as part of a celebration of their coming of age. Celebrations often include special foods, guests, music, and sometimes a parade in honor of the male child who is now considered a young man. The coming of age for a female may not be recognized with the fanfare of a male in many Muslim areas, but the beginning of modest dress, including veiling in some areas, is a clear sign to the community that the child is now a young woman. Some Muslim countries practice a controversial operation called the clitoridectomy or female circumcision. The practice has been outlawed in most Western countries but is still observed in certain parts of the world. It is done with the intent of minimalizing the sexual drive of the female, which supposedly assists her in her attempt to lead a virtuous life. Some Hadiths support this practice while other Hadiths condemn the practice.

As mentioned earlier in this chapter, Muhammad encouraged men and women to marry and have families. Marriages bring the community together and are celebrated over several days. Many Muslim areas still arrange marriages with a contract that must be agreed upon by the groom and the family of the bride. These legal contracts may include demands such as a certain number of children, a specific location of the home, the expected level of lifestyle, or any other items agreed upon by both parties. The signing of a marriage contract is an important event that begins the preparation for the marriage. Although males from the bride's family represent her in the negotiations, the bride is supposed to agree to whatever is specified in the marriage contract. As mentioned earlier, the groom is expected to pay a bride price, and the goods provided are to be set aside for the protection of the bride. One controversial form of marriage that has been outlawed in most Muslim countries but is allowed in many Shi'ite communities is the temporary marriage. A temporary marriage is one established for a fixed period of time between a man and a woman. The man is required to provide some type of bride price, although the amount is much less than the regular bride price. Also mentioned earlier, a man can marry a concubine or female slave without being subject to the limitation of four wives stipulated in Islamic law.

The final key event in the life cycle relates to a death in the community. Just as a birth is celebrated as an expansion of the community, a death is viewed as a great loss. Unlike death rituals in the West, Muslims do not embalm the bodies of the dead. Thus, they usually bury the bodies within thirty-six hours of death. Mourning is allowed and even expected, but excessive mourning is not encouraged nor considered acceptable in many places. Among Shi'ites, mourning may be a particularly emotional experience, especially when one mourns a great saint of Islam. Traditional burials may include placing the coffin sideways in the grave so that the individual will face in the direction of Mecca. Because funerals are detrimental to the community, they are usually simple ceremonies that include important religious rituals such as performing the *salat* and Qur'anic recitation. During mourning, no jewelry or perfume is worn, and mourners often wear unwashed clothes as a sign of grief. Muslims may mourn from a few days to a few months depending on their local custom; after this time, the person is to rejoin the ranks of the remaining community.

Life in the Muslim Community

The literal center of all Muslim communities is the mosque. All Muslims in the area can hear the call to prayer throughout the day. Muslims often use the mosque for the daily prayers, although many pray in other locations. The key event of the mosque is the Friday Prayer Service in which the Muslim community gathers for the noon prayer and to hear a message from the leader of the mosque, or the Imam. Each mosque contains the area used for prayer, often an open area with carpets in roofed mosques, and an area used for purification or washing prior to the performing of the prayers. Some mosques are open-air areas with concrete floors. Beyond prayer, the mosque provides many other services for the community. The mosque is often a key educational station where children or adults can learn portions of the Qur'an and hear lessons taught on important Qur'anic texts. Some mosques are associated with the training of those who lead in the call to prayer (muezzin) and the training of mosque leaders or Imams. Mosques can be a social gathering point for the community, a place of refuge in times of turmoil, and even a medical facility when the community is engaged in a military conflict. Some mosques are part of a larger structure, often called an Islamic center, that contains a large collection of books on Islamic history, teachings, and life.

Two other important gathering places for Muslims around the world are the marketplace and the tea or coffee shop. In the marketplace, fresh foods and other goods can be purchased. Often the marketplace is located near the mosque area. Usually the market area closest to the mosque is where shoppers can find items used in the practice of Islam such as a copy of the Qur'an, prayer beads, and other items. The coffee or tea shop is also an important gathering place where individuals can relax and engage in casual conversation. Some Muslims drink hot tea, while others prefer hot coffee. These oases can also provide an environment for a friendly game of backgammon or chess. Typically, one finds primarily males in the coffee or tea shops throughout the Muslim world. Although the taste of the tea or coffee may differ from place to place, the importance of these locations as a vital part of community building is universal.

Behavior in these public places may seem somewhat unusual to many from North America and Europe. The dress of males and females reflects a cultural value of modesty. Men often wear loose-fitting outfits that are comfortable in the warm areas, and they often don distinctive headwear that may differ from place to place. Women are encouraged, and in some places required, to dress modestly, which often means covering the whole body except the eyes. The goal of dressing modestly is to convey religious piety and to avoid dressing to stir the wandering eye of the opposite sex. In many Muslim, countries eye contact between men and women who are not married is not considered acceptable. Many from the West have difficulty with this tradition because making eye contact is viewed as necessary for building trust. An American male attempting to make eye contact with a Muslim female may be perceived as making a sexual overture, and the same is true of American females attempting to make eye contact with Muslim males. For Muslims in North America and Europe, the issue of eye contact may not be as much of an offense as in traditional Muslim societies around the world. Another big adjustment for Westerners who journey to Muslim areas is public displays of affection. Husbands and wives usually do not make public displays of affection, but physical contact between men or between women is common. One may see two men or two women holding hands while having a friendly conversation. This gesture is simply a display of friendship and has nothing to do with sexual orientation. Also, meetings between men or between women may include a three-kiss greeting alternating between the right and left cheek.

Many from the West may consider the life of a Muslim in Egypt or Jordan as somber, but Muslims do take time to enjoy one another's company. Friends may share a meal together, drink coffee or tea together, or play a game of chess or backgammon. Traditional hobbies or activities throughout the history of Islam have included horseback riding, archery, and table games. Both watching and playing sports are acceptable forms of entertainment. Soccer and basketball are popular sports in many Muslim areas. Movies are an acceptable form of entertainment if their content does not conflict with the values of Islam. Smoking is common in most Muslim areas. Cigarettes and water pipes are commonly found in Muslim countries around the globe.

Islamic Holidays and Festivals

In addition to celebrations representing cycle-of-life events such as the birth of a child, a child's coming of age, and marriage between a man and woman, the community celebrates annual events to recognize the yearly cycle observed by Muslims. The first of the observances is the celebration of the new year. This celebration recognizes the gift of another year from God and also signifies the beginning of the Muslim calendar through the remembering of the journey of Muhammad from Mecca to Medina in 622. The Muslim New Year's Day begins a ten-day celebration that culminates with the Ashura, which functions like the Jewish celebration of Yom Kippur or Day of Atonement. A Muslim tradition held that Muhammad observed Jews fasting on this day to remember God's leading Moses and the Hebrews out of Egypt as Pharaoh finally granted their release. The tradition holds that Muhammad called upon Muslims to fast on that day (al-Bukhair). This time of the year is both a celebration and a preparation for the upcoming year. The Shi'ites use this period as a time of mourning because on the day of Ashura, the son of Ali, Husayn, was killed by Umayyad troops as he attempted to revolt against their imperial rule. Husain's martyrdom is reenacted through a type of passion play that attempts to honor his heroic death. Some Muslims also celebrate the ark of Noah coming to rest on Mount Ararat, the birth of Abraham, and the establishment of Ka'ba on this day.

During the third month of the Muslim year, the Muslims celebrate the birth of the prophet Muhammad. The celebration of Muhammad's birthday probably did not begin until the thirteenth century when Muslims felt a need to honor him and his contributions to the Muslim community. Although Muhammad's birth is celebrated in some Muslim countries, Muslims in other places consider such a celebration as idolatrous because of the danger of elevating Muhammad to a status that goes beyond his role as prophet.

During the seventh month of the Islamic calendar Rajeb, Muslims celebrate and remember the Mi'raj or the Night Journey of Muhammad to Jerusalem and to the seven levels of heaven. Muslims hold that Muhammad was transported from Mecca to Jerusalem and ascended into the seven levels of heaven from the al-Aqsa mosque, which today is near the site of the Dome of the Rock mosque. Muslim tradition holds that the rock that lies below the Dome of the Rock is the one upon which Abraham was prepared to offer his son Ishmael, but God spared Ishmael and a ram was offered in his stead. While traveling through these levels, according to Islamic tradition, Muhammad met Abraham, Moses, and Jesus. From this journey, Muhammad established the *salat* or daily prayers much as they are observed today.

The eighth month called Sha'aban serves as a time of preparation for the month-long fast. To prepare for the fast, Muslims are to seek forgiveness for any grievances with others. Muslims may choose to fast during this month to prepare themselves, but only if it would not jeopardize their ability to fulfill the month-long fast during Ramadan. In the middle of the month is one holy night called "the night of freedom from fire" in which persons seek forgiveness from God. On this Night of Forgiveness, Muslims are not only to seek forgiveness from God, but also to resolve any conflicts with other Muslims. The activities of this night may include the performing of a night prayer, reciting the Qur'an, reciting the name of Allah, and praying personally for particular situations facing individual Muslims and their communities. Some Muslims may spend the entire night performing these activities. The purpose of this night and the entire eighth month is the preparation for the month-long fast during Ramadan.

The ninth month of the year is the month of Ramadan when Muslims are to fast from the time the sun rises until the sun sets. The fast includes avoiding both food and drink during the daylight hours to remind each Muslim of his or her dependence upon God. Other restrictions, described in chapter 3, are also to be observed during the daily fast. The purpose of the fast is not merely to avoid food and other detractions, but to reflect upon God, become more dedicated to God, and develop self-control. Some also suggest that the fast reminds the community of the needs of those less fortunate so that they might be thankful for what they have and be generous to those in need. Late in the month of Ramadan is the Night of Power, a special, powerful night for prayer. Muslims around the world may spend this entire night praying as a culmination of the reflections of the month. Shi'ites also celebrate the naming of Ali as Muhammad's successor during the month of Ramadan.

The first three days of the tenth month Shawwal celebrate the ending of the month-long fast, and friends and family gather to share in a great feast. The lessons learned and the devotion gained during Ramadan are to provide a context of dedication to personal piety and communal responsibility.

The twelfth month of the Muslim calendar Dhu al-Hijjah is the month of the pilgrimage to Mecca. At least once in the life of every Muslim, he or she should journey to Mecca during the month of the pilgrimage to commemorate the sacrifice of Abraham. The details of the pilgrimage can be found in chapter 3. Those who do not journey to Mecca during the month of pilgrimage often offer the sacrifice of a ram in their own communities to celebrate the sacrifice of Abraham.[1]

Summary

The goal of these festivals, rituals, and celebrations is to remind individual Muslims of their blessings and responsibilities to God and to each other. These events also serve to unite the community so that it may fulfill its purpose to be God's faithful agents upon the earth to honor God and serve God faithfully as one unified body.

---

[1] For an overview of the Muslim calendar, see Cyril Glassé, *The Concise Encyclopedia of Islam* (New York: HarperCollins Publishers, 1989) 81–84.

Chapter 10

A PICTURE OF
MUSLIM-CHRISTIAN RELATIONS

Before addressing Islam's relationship to Christianity, one must consider Islam's relationship to Judaism. Throughout the book, the reader can see that Judaism and Islam have linguistic connections, as Arabic and Hebrew are of the same language family. Both Jews and Arabs view Abraham as their biological and spiritual ancestor. Both express prayers each day: Muslims five times per day and Jews three times per day. Jerusalem is considered a holy city for both religions, and both esteem people like Moses, David, and Elijah. Both religions share a dedication to the laws revealed in their books and both see the hand of God at work in their history. Jews and Muslims both see themselves as monotheists or believing in one God. Many other similarities exist between the two religions, but they part in that the Muslims recognize Muhammad as a prophet from God and consider the Qur'an a revelation from God whereas Judaism does not. Judaism existed in Arabia during the time of Muhammad, and he invited Jews to join him in creating one monotheistic religion, but their rejection of Muhammad's authority led to battles between the Islamic community and Jewish tribes.

Christianity also shares many common points with Islam. Both religions esteem Jerusalem as a holy city and recognize the importance of people like Moses, David, and Jesus. Christians and Muslims share a vision that their religion is universal and not limited by one's ethnic identity. Both believe a Day of Judgment will one day occur and that persons will either enter into heaven or hell. Christians were present in Arabia at the time of Muhammad, and like the Jews they were invited to join Muhammad and the Muslim community. Jews and Christians were called "people of the book" because Muhammad believed that each group had revealed Scriptures to follow. Yet in the end Muslims criticized Christians because they, like the Jews, did not recognize the Qur'an as the revelation of God and Muhammad as God's prophet. In this chapter, the reader will first consider a brief historical perspective of the relationship between Muslims and Christians. Next is a presentation on some of the shared and divergent teachings of both religions. Finally, the chapter will conclude with a description of the greatest barriers for a positive relationship between Muslims and Christians.

Historical Perspectives

After Muhammad and the Muslims took control of Arabia, Christians and Jews were allowed to continue living in the land in exchange for a tax that would provide protection in times of war, as they were not allowed to fight in the same army as the Muslims. The same held true as Islam expanded into the areas once held by the Christian Byzantine Empire. At different times in Islamic history, Christians have played important roles in places like Bagdad (Iraq) and Cordova (Spain).

One of the earliest records of a Christian response to Islam came through the writings of John of Damascus in the eighth century. He considered Islam to be a Christian heresy rather than a separate religion that developed in Arabia. He considered Muhammad to be immoral and the Qur'an to be a creation of Muhammad to justify his immoral lifestyle. Although few sources exist that discuss the Christian response to the development of the Muslim community, the attitudes of John of Damascus were probably fairly representative of many Christians at the time. One of the reasons for such a conclusion draws from centuries of Rome combating groups like the Gnostics and Monophysites as heresies. Later writers like Dante applauded the Muslim philosophers but wrote stinging remarks about Muhammad and Ali.

The Crusades

The single most recorded period of Christian-Muslim relations took place during the time of the Crusades. Space prevents a thorough examination of the Crusades, but what follows is a picture or glimpse of their impact on Muslim-Christian relations. The fact that Muslims had entered and taken control of the holy city of Jerusalem stirred the hearts of many Christians in Europe. An effort to take back Jerusalem and other holy cities became a major objective by the end of the eleventh century. The Crusades represented the desire both to take back holy lands and to retrieve holy relics from the earliest followers of Christianity and even Jesus himself. The motivation for the Crusades probably combined religious duty and political expediency due to the fact that church and state were ultimately linked together. What was perceived as good for the state was good for the church, and what was good for the church was good for the state.[1] One could argue that political expansion and building a military reputation were as strong a motive as the protection of holy sites and holy relics.

The first Crusade began in 1095 in response to a passionate plea by Pope Urban II, who called for the retaking of holy land and especially the city of Jerusalem from the Turks. Fighting battles along the way, the Crusaders marched toward Jerusalem wearing uniforms emblazoned with their symbol of the cross. In 1099 they were able to take control of Jerusalem as they pushed the Muslim army back. Some records point to attacks on Jewish areas during the first Crusade. The taking of Jerusalem was a bloody affair and is recorded in the writings of Raymond d'Aguilers. Once Jerusalem was captured, Godfrey Bouillon was named as the first Christian king of the city.

By 1144, the Muslim armies were pushing their way back into these holy lands, and the response was a second Crusade in 1145. The king of France joined the efforts of defending Jerusalem and the surrounding lands against Muslim invaders, but the attempt failed to prevent the fall of Jerusalem to the exploits of Saladin. Saladin's taking of Jerusalem led to another Crusade that included three of Europe's famous kings (Richard the Lionhearted, Frederick Barbarossa, and Philip II) as they attempted to regain control of the city. This effort failed, as they could not take control of the entirety of Jerusalem. The holding of Jerusalem by Christians or Muslims seemed to symbolize the power and legitimacy of their respective religions.

---

[1] Motives for the crusaders are discussed in Karen Armstrong's *Holy War: The Crusades and Their Impact on Today's World*, 2nd ed. (New York: Anchor Books, 2001) 153.

A fourth Crusade was organized in 1202–1204 to take back the city of Constantinople, the capital of the Eastern or Byzantine Empire, which had fallen to the Turks. The Crusaders were able to take back the city for a period of about sixty years until it fell permanently into Muslim hands. Eventually, it would be renamed Istanbul.

A fifth Crusade took place from 1217–1221 as the Crusaders attempted to take control of Egypt. During this Crusade, St. Francis of Assisi traveled with the Crusaders to meet with the sultan of Egypt in an attempt to reach him with love rather than violence. Remarkably, St. Francis was granted an audience with the Muslim leader. Sources vary greatly on the impact of this meeting, but regardless of the direct outcome, the meeting represents one of the first recorded efforts of Christians to reach Muslims with a method other than warfare. The remaining Crusades were not as well organized, and all of them failed to achieve their goals. Some suggest that the Crusade led by Frederick II was the last (1227–1229), while others suggest another Crusade, organized by King Louis IX (1245–1247), ended the period of the Crusades.

For Europe, the Crusades ended in the thirteenth century during the medieval period of European history. The events of the Protestant Reformation, the Roman Catholic Counter-Reformation, and the Enlightenment relegated the Crusades to ancient history. Yet for many Muslims, any effort on the part of Europeans and North Americans to interfere with Muslim-held territories was perceived as a continuation of the medieval Crusades.

Missionary Efforts

As mentioned above, St. Francis of Assisi's (1181–1226) visit with Egypt's sultan represented one of the first recorded missionary efforts of Christians attempting to reach Muslims. He sought to provide a missionary approach to Islam rather than a forceful one. His efforts were followed by individuals like Raymond Lull (1233–1315), who attempted to reach Muslims in North Africa by love and prayer as an alternative to violence. Although Lull's method focused on nonviolence, his words were harsh against Muhammad and the teachings of Islam. Lull led the effort of making a study of the Arabic language, and Islamic culture available in European universities.[2]

In the fifteenth century, the Spanish theologian John of Segovia continued the argument against the use of violence and sought to use a form of intellectual disputation to reach Muslims. He attempted to organize a Muslim-Christian conference, but the event never took place because he died on the journey to meet with the Turkish leader who had taken charge of Constantinople.[3] John also translated the Qur'an into Latin to make it available for a European study of the text. Around the same time, Nicholas of Cusa penned a book that

---

[2] For a good description of Raymond Lull, see Kenneth Scott Latourette's *A History of the Expansion of Christianity*, vol. 2 (Grand Rapids MI: Zondervan Publishing Company, 1938) 321–24. See also Ruth A. Tucker, *From Jerusalem to Irian Jaya: A Biographical History of Christian Missions* (Grand Rapids MI: Zondervan Publishing Company, 1983) 52–57.

[3] *Biographical Dictionary of Christian Missions*, ed. Gerald H. Anderson (Grand Rapids MI: William B. Eerdmans Publishing Company, 1998) 335.

created an imaginary dialogue between the religions of his day and attempted to portray the common themes and differences between these religions. The pope asked him to write a book, *Sifting of the Qur'an*, that focused on the differences between Christianity and Islam and provided material by which Christians could refute errors in the teachings of Islam.[4] Although Cusa's attitude toward Islam seemed positive, some have suggested that he supported a crusade against the Turks when Rome deemed it necessary.[5]

A few years later the reformer Martin Luther (1483–1546) articulated a rather staunch attitude toward the Turks, who were battling with European powers at the time. Luther wrote, "The Turks have retained many features of the law of Moses, but, inflated with the insolence of victory, they have adapted a new worship, for the glory of warlike triumph is, in the opinion of the world, the greatest of all."[6] Luther also referred to the Turks as the "devil incarnate."[7] Additionally, he severely criticized the Qur'an as a threat to the Christian faith.[8]

In his *Inferno*, Dante shared Luther's harsh rhetoric, depicting Muhammad and Ali in the lower reaches of hell because they caused a schism or split.[9] Some writers have

---

[4] See Charles Kimball, *Striving Together: A Way Forward in Christian-Muslim Relations* (Maryknoll NY: Orbis Books, 1991) 42.

[5] *Biographical Dictionary*, ed. Anderson, 494.

[6] Martin Luther, "Of the Turks," in *The Table-Talk of Martin Luther*, trans, William Hazlitt (Philadelphia: The Lutheran Publication Society, reprint of the 1848 ed.).

[7] Martin Luther, *Luther's Works*, vol. 46, ed. Jaroslav Pelikan (Saint Louis MO: Concordia Publishing Company, 1955) 181.

[8] Ibid., 176–82.

[9] Dante Alighieri, *Inferno*, trans. Michael Palma (New York: W. W. Norton & Company, 2002) 313.

suggested that Dante believed Muhammad and Ali to be members of a Christian heretical group rather than a monotheist in the midst of a polytheistic society.[10]

Henry Martyn (1781–1812) was a gifted linguist and Bible translator. The Cambridge-trained missionary and chaplain translated the New Testament into several Indian languages, Arabic, and Persian. On a visit to Iran to check the accuracy of his Persian translation, he met with important Muslim religious leaders. This encounter led to the sharing of religious tracts and to the eventual publication of his *Controversial Tracts on Christianity and Muhammadans*.[11] He died young, but his legacy is reflected in a number of programs that use his name today. Late in the nineteenth century, another important scholar, Samuel Zwemer, helped provide an understanding of Islam to Western Christians. Zwemer, sometimes called the apostle to Islam, lived thirty-eight years in Arabia and Egypt as a teacher and missionary. His intellectual savvy led to him taking a teaching post at Princeton Theological Seminary and to his establishing *Muslim World* as a journal to provide Christians in the West with an understanding of Islam. Zwemer proved to be a prolific writer, completing twenty-nine books and co-authoring nineteen others.[12] Most of his writings focused on Islam, and his name is associated with institutions that have a focus on Islamic studies.

An interesting Christian scholar of Islam, Louis Massignon, emerged early in the twentieth century. Massignon studied some of the earliest Muslim mystics and taught at the famous College de France in Paris. His studies moved him to

---

[10] Ibid. See the footnote for l. 31 on p. 320.
[11] *Biographical Dictionary*, ed. Anderson, 438.
[12] Ibid., 763.

be more dedicated as a Christian, and he established a spiritual society based on prayer.[13] Another important scholar came from the Anglican church in the person of Kenneth Cragg. Cragg served as an Anglican priest, church pastor, missionary, bishop, and professor. He trained in Islamic studies at Oxford University with a focus on contemporary Islam. He lived a number of years in Beirut, Jerusalem, and Cairo, which provided a context for ministry and research.

Cragg taught at several institutions in the United Kingdom, Nigeria, and the United States. He served as the editor of *Muslim World* while he taught at the Hartford Seminary Foundation. His works are prolific and provide one of the best understandings of Islam by a Christian writer.[14] His works include *The Call of the Minaret, Sandals in the Mosque: Christian Presence Amidst Islam, The Event of the Qur'an*, and a thematic collection from the Qur'an called *Readings in the Qur'an.*

The bottom line is that after the Crusades, Christians began attempting to minister to Muslims in their respective countries. The approaches ranged from debate as missionaries challenged the piety of Muhammad and the authenticity of the Qur'an to the use of reason and service in an effort to dialogue with Muslims. Today both approaches can be found with equal commitment.[15] Two large organizations continue to address

---

[13] Ibid., 440.

[14] Ibid., 157.

[15] For more information regarding the history of Christian-Muslim relations, see Charles Kimball, *Striving Together: A Way Forward in Christian-Muslim Relations* (Maryknoll NY: Orbis Books, 1991), and George W. Braswell Jr., *Islam: Its Prophet, Peoples, Politics, and Power* (Nashville: Broadman and Holman Publishers, 1996).

the appropriate approach to Muslims around the world, the World Council of Churches and the Lausanne Committee for World Evangelization. Although their approaches may differ, these groups seek to minister to Muslims around the world peaceably in an effort to be a genuine witness for God through Jesus Christ.

Jesus

Christians are named as such because they view themselves as followers or disciples of Jesus Christ. Christian tradition holds fast to the belief that only one God exists and that the one and only God chose to enter into history in the person of Jesus of Nazareth. According to Christianity, Jesus was the fulfillment of the Old Testament prophecies concerning the Messiah, which is why Jesus is known as Jesus Christ ("Christ" is the Greek translation of the Hebrew term "Messiah"). Christians around the world would cringe at the notion that they are polytheists, yet because of the concept of the trinity, many Muslims consider Christians to be polytheists. Instead of the Christian teaching that one God is manifested as Father, Son, and Holy Spirit, many Muslims consider Christian theology to be the promotion of at least three gods. This issue is addressed again later in the chapter.

Whom do Muslims understand Jesus to be? Jesus is mentioned in 11 of the 114 chapters of the Qur'an. Jesus is considered to be a prophet who received a book or revelation from God, which the Qur'an calls the Injil or Gospel. The following is a Qur'anic presentation of Jesus.

According to the Qur'an, Jesus was born as the son of the virgin Mary (Surah 19:20; 3:47) and was to be called Christ Jesus (3:45–47). The miracles of Jesus began early in his life; he was able to identify himself as a servant of God who had been given a revelation and made a prophet of God (19:29–34), and as a child, he made a bird out of clay and brought it to life by breathing into it (3:49; 5:113). Jesus is called a righteous prophet (6:85) who was given the Injil or Gospel (5:49). According to the Qur'an, Jesus had disciples who were faithful Muslims (3:52–53) and shared a table with Jesus, possibly a reference to the Lord's Supper (5:114–118). Jesus, according to the Qur'an, is a witness and sign for the Day of Judgment (4:159; 43:61) and provides the same message as the other prophets (3:84–86). Jesus is described as being like Adam (3:59) and confirming the law given to Moses (61:6). In the Qur'an, Jesus performs miracles during his adult years including healing the blind and lepers and raising the dead (5:113–18). God also raises Jesus up (3:55; 4:158). Most of these teachings of the Qur'an do not directly conflict with the Christian portrayal of the life of Jesus, although some of the childhood stories are not found in the Gospels.

Some descriptions of Jesus in the Qur'an conflict with his descriptions in the four Gospels. According to the Qur'an, Jesus did not die on the cross but only appeared to do so (4:157). The Qur'an states that Jesus is no more than a prophet or apostle (4:171; 5:78; 43:59, 63–64). It further states that those who say God is Christ are committing blasphemy (5:19, 75) and that Jesus is not the son of God (9:30–31). Jesus and Mary are not to be worshipped, according to the Qur'an (5:119–20). One reference to Jesus in the Qur'an has him predicting the coming of Ahmad, which many Muslims believe is a reference to Muhammad; Christians hold that this is Jesus' prediction of the coming of the Holy Spirit (61:6).

In addition to the Qur'anic teachings concerning Jesus, many Hadith or Islamic traditions list other activities or characteristics of Jesus. According to an al-Bukhari Hadith, all persons are born sinners, except Jesus. Other Hadith materials point to the role of Jesus in the final judgment, and some even point to the premise that Jesus will return to the earth again to marry and have children.

Overall, Muslims respect Jesus as an apostle of Islam who received a revelation from God (Injil). Although many miracles are associated with Jesus, Muslims suggest that the focus should be on his message rather than his miracles. The message of Jesus was to worship God alone and prepare for the Day of Judgment. Muslims hold that Jesus never claimed to be equal with God and that later Christians such as Paul contributed to this mistaken notion. Most Muslims believe Jesus did not die on the cross but was instead raised up by God. Many of the teachings of Christianity such as the necessity of the crucifixion, justification by faith, and others are the inventions of Paul, according to many Muslims. Jesus plays an important role in Islam, but even though the Qur'an portrays Christians as the nearest to Muslims in love (5:85), most Muslims consider the Christian teachings concerning Jesus to be corrupted.[16] Perhaps the Qur'an offers the best description of the Muslim position on the teachings of Jesus:

---

[16] For more information concerning the view of Jesus in the Qur'an and in Islam, see Geoffrey Parrinder, *Jesus in the Qur'an* (Oxford: Oneworld Publications, 1995), and *The Muslim Jesus: Sayings and Stories in Islamic Literature*, ed. and trans. Tarif Khalidi (Cambridge MA: Harvard University Press, 2001).

O People of the Book! Commit no excesses in your religion; nor say of God aught but the truth. Christ Jesus the son of Mary was (no more than) an apostle of God, and His Word, which he bestowed on Mary, and a Spirit proceeding from Him: so believe in God and His apostles. Say not "Trinity": desist: it will be better for you: for God is One God: glory be to Him (Far Exalted is He) above having a son. To Him belong all things in the heavens and on earth. And enough is God as a Disposer of affairs.[17]

I have attempted to point out the similarities and the differences between Islam and Christianity. The last portion of the chapter focuses on some of the key issues that create barriers to the establishment of positive Muslim-Christian relations, both in the West and in Muslim countries around the world. The issues include political, social, and religious topics.

Top Ten Barriers in Muslim-Christian Relations

These barriers are not intended to be ranked from most important to least important; rather, they simply are ten barriers that hinder Muslim-Christian relations. One is ignorance. Few Christians have made an effort to try to understand Islam in its cultural and historical context. Likewise, few Muslims have made an effort to understand Christianity in its cultural and historical context. The result of this lack of effort is that Muslims and Christians around the world treat assumptions and stereotypes as facts. Many

[17] Surah 4:171.

Christians assume that all Muslims teach that they should worship Muhammad the way Christians worship Jesus, but this is not a teaching of Islam. Many Muslims believe Christians teach that God came down to earth and impregnated Mary to produce a god-man in the tradition of Hercules, but this is not a teaching of Christianity. As long as stereotypes are treated as facts, the divide of ignorance will separate Muslims and Christians.

A second barrier in Muslim-Christian relations is legitimacy. The inability or unwillingness of Muslims to accept Jesus Christ as God in human form and to accept the Bible as we have it today offends Christian. For Muslims, Christianity is an illegitimate religion that fails to honor the one true God of the universe. The inability or unwillingness of Christians to recognize that Muhammad is a prophet of God and the Qur'an is the revealed word of God offends Muslims. For Christians, Islam is an illegitimate religion that fails to honor the one true God of the universe. Legitimacy creates an environment of competition between Christianity and Islam because proponents of both religions feel that they have a universal appeal for the whole world.

A third barrier to Muslim-Christian relations is history. The Crusades represent a painful chapter for both Muslims and Christians. Beyond the Crusades, European powers colonized many Muslim lands. During colonization, Muslims lived under Western domination, which they equated with Christian domination; thus, the traditions of the Crusades continued in the eyes of many Muslims. The globalization of the economy, driven by the West, has changed the daily life of many Muslims. Some see this as progress, while others view these changes as a challenge to their traditional existence.

Although some positive relations can be found between Muslims and Christians, for the most part both histories are filled with conflict.

A fourth barrier to Muslim-Christian relations is theology. Both religions consider themselves to be monotheistic, and both see Abraham as a pillar of faith, yet Islam rejects the concept of the trinity. One stereotype that exists in some Muslim areas is that Christians worship three gods—Father, Son, and Mother (Mary)—or that Christians believe Jesus is half god and half man. Christians believe God chose to enter human history as a human being named Jesus. The thought that God would do such a thing challenges the lofty view of God held by most Muslims. Christians often stereotype Muslims as worshipping Muhammad, but even though Muhammad is highly respected, no Muslim would say that he worships Muhammad. The role of Jesus compares to the role of the Qur'an, not to that of Muhammad. For the Christian, the clearest picture of God is found in Jesus, whereas the clearest picture of God for the Muslim is the Qur'an. The Bible is the avenue by which Christians view Jesus, and Muhammad is the avenue by which Muslims view the Qur'an.

A fifth barrier to Muslim-Christian relations is the fact that both religions see themselves as the one true religion that appeals to people all over the world. Because both consider their religion to be universal in its appeal, they both consider mission activity to be an essential component of their faith. Simply put, Muslims see Islam as a global religion, and they have missionaries serving around the world to spread the message of Islam. Christians, likewise, consider Christianity to be a global religion, and they have missionaries serving around the world to spread the message of the gospel. The mission activity of each religions is often viewed as a threat to the vitality and appeal of the other tradition. In other words, Muslim converts to Christianity are viewed as a loss to Islam, and Christian converts to Islam are viewed similarly. Members of each religion equate the mission activity of the other religion as a competition for the faith of the world.

A sixth barrier to Muslim-Christian relations is Israel. Sometimes the relationship between the Jews and Muslims is described as two brothers fighting over their father's inheritance. The emotional energy of two brothers fighting can exceed the battling of two strangers. The creation of the modern state of Israel in 1948 by the Western nations through the Balfour Declaration intended to provide a homeland for Jews following the Holocaust of World War II. The impact for many Muslims was that Christian nations established the modern state of Israel as a slap in the face of the Arab Muslims living in Palestine. By implication, recognizing the legitimacy of Israel is perceived by many Muslims as a rejection of the legitimacy of claims of the Palestinians who are, for the most part, Muslims.

A seventh barrier to Muslim-Christian relations is culture. Western Christians, as a result of the Protestant Reformation and the Enlightenment, focus on the significance of the individual. As reflected in the movie *Saving Private Ryan*, each person is important. This film portrays several soldiers who risk their lives in order to save the life of one man after his brothers are all killed in action. Many Muslims consider the theme of this movie to be foolhardy in principle because the life of one soldier is not worth the risk of losing several lives. The survival of the community, for Islam, is more important than any one soldier. Because the group is more important than the individual, one can understand the willingness of a single Muslim to volunteer for a suicide bombing mission in an effort to defend the survival of the Muslim community.

An eighth barrier to Muslim-Christian relations is church-state relations. During the medieval period of European history, the church and state were intimately intertwined, but that changed over time. The state and church became separated, with each having its distinctive role. Although many European nations still have a strong church-state relationship, for the most part the church functions apart from the state and vice versa. The first amendment of the United States Constitution provides for the freedom of religion from state interference and is considered an enigma to many Muslims, who hold that the state and religious community are both accountable to God. Islam emerged as a religious and political force, and to separate religion from politics seems to be an unnatural, if not an unhealthy concept for many Muslims. Thus, many Muslims perceive the actions and statements of the United States government as the exploits of Christian America. For this reason, the use of Crusader language is a powerful motivating tool used by radical Muslims today. When British or United States political leaders use words like "crusade," "invasion," and other words commonly used by Crusaders during medieval times, they provide fodder for Muslim radicals who use these words to convince their audience that the West is on a crusade against Islam, not against terrorism.

A ninth barrier to Muslim-Christian relations is language. Christianity and Islam share many common religious words, such as "sin" and "mercy." For Christians, sins are to be confessed to God through Jesus Christ, but for the Muslim obedience and righteous living are the means to deal with sinful actions. In Christianity, Jesus serves as the intercessor between God and the Christian, while Islam proclaims that no one can serve as an intercessor. The Qur'an declares that no one can intercede between God and humanity. For the Christian, mercy is displayed in the willingness of Jesus to die on the cross as an act of redemption, but for the Muslim, mercy belongs to God, and God will show mercy on whomever God chooses to show mercy. Although similar words are used in both traditions, the meanings of these words may differ greatly.

The tenth barrier to Muslim-Christian relations is propaganda. Western nations have taken care to describe their military activities following the events of September 11, 2001, as action against terrorism and not an attack on Islam. Revivalists carefully use words like "Crusades" to evoke the emotions of people, arguing that any military activity that involves a Western military is indeed an attack on Islam. Revivalists often represent persons who are self-taught and who lack higher education, but they do not lack in their ability to use emotion-laden propaganda to achieve the desired effect. Propaganda is not the exclusive property of Muslim Revivalists, as Western nations sometimes report events in the Muslim world that do nothing to overcome the stereotype that all Muslims are radical terrorists.[18] The invasion of Iraq revealed the power of the media to portray a particular image

---

[18] For a Pakistani Christian perspective on Islam, see Michael Nazir-Ali, *Islam: A Christian Perspective* (Philadelphia: Westminster Press, 1983). For an excellent discussion of Christian and Muslim images and meanings, see Kenneth Cragg, *The Call of the Minaret* (New York: Oxford University Press, 1964), and David W. Shenk, *Journeys of the Muslim Nation and the Christian Church: Exploring the Mission of the Two Communities* (Scottsdale PA: Herald Press, 2003).

of a world event. While CNN was showing statues of Saddam Hussein crashing to the ground and Iraqis cheering their newfound freedom, some Arab news reports showed children with missing limbs as their image of the invasion.

Summary

The goal of this volume has not been to present a comprehensive survey of Islam, but to present pictures of Islam that enable the reader to see the complexities of Islam as expressed throughout the world. The author of this manuscript is a committed Christian and affirms the tenants of Christianity, yet the author recognizes that many of the problems facing the world today are due to a lack of understanding. Muslims represent a diverse group of people who share a common heritage but also differ greatly on some key issues facing the world today. My hope is that the information will provide a glimpse into the lives, history, and traditions of Muslims around the world so that stereotypes can be replaced with, at least, a partial understanding of Islam. Differences between Christianity and Islam will always exist, but at least the differences should be based on a reasonable understanding of the other religion. In a day and age when emotions run high, the hope is that Christians can respond to the Islam that exists rather than an Islam that is generated from Western Media. I have been challenged in my own study of Islam to dedicate myself to be more faithful in my pilgrimage as a Christian and as a Christian minister. I hope that these pictures of Islam have enabled you better to understand the world of the religion of Islam and the people called Muslims.

BIBLIOGRAPhY

Reference Works

Bearman, P. J., et al., editors. *Encyclopaedia of Islam*. Twelve volumes with supplements. Leiden: E. J. Brill, 2005.

Gibb, H. A. R., and J. II. Kramers. *Shorter Encyclopaedia of Islam*. Ithaca NY: Cornell University Press, 1965.

Glassé, Cyril. *The New Encyclopedia of Islam*. Lanham MD: Altamira Press, 2001.

Introductions

Cragg, Kenneth, and R. Marston Speight. *The House of Islam*. Third edition. Belmont CA: Wadsworth Publishing Company, 1988.

Denny, Frederick Mathewson. *An Introduction to Islam*. Third edition. Upper Saddle River NJ: Pearson Prentice-Hall, 2006.

Nasr, Seyyed Hossein. *Islam: Religion, History, and Civilization*. New York: HarperCollins Publishers, 2003.

Nazir-Ali, Michael. *Islam: A Christian Perspective*. Philadelphia: The Westminster Press, 1983.

Rahman, Fazlur. *Islam*. Second edition. Chicago: University of Chicago Press, 1979.

Tritton, A. S. *Islam*. London: Hutchinson University Library, 1951.

Pre-Islamic Arabia

Hitti, Phillip K. *History of the Arabs*. Ninth edition. New York: St. Martin's Press, 1967.

Hourani, Albert. *A History of the Arab Peoples*. London: Faber and Faber Limited, 1991.

Muhammad

Ibn Ishaq,. *The Life of Muhammad*. Translated by A. Guillaume. New York: Oxford University Press, 1955.
Watt, W. Montgomery. *Muhammad at Mecca*. London: Oxford University Press, 1953.
———. *Muhammad at Medina*. London: Oxford University Press, 1956.
———. *Muhammad: Prophet and Statesman*. London: Oxford University Press, 1961.

The Qur'an (Translations)

Ali, A. Yusuf. *The Holy Qur'an: Text, Translation and Commentary*. Brentwood MD: Amana Corporation, 1989.
Arberry, A. J. *The Koran Interpreted*. London: Allen & Unwin, 1955.
Cragg, Kenneth. *Readings in the Qur'an*. Brighton: Sussex Academic Press, 1999.
Dawood, N. J. *The Koran: With a Parallel Arabic Text*. New York: Viking Penguin, 1990.
Pickthall, Mohammad Marmaduke. *The Meaning of the Glorious Koran: An Explanatory Translation*. New York: Mentor Books, n.d.
Sells, Michael. *Approaching the Qur'an: The Early Revelations*. Ashland OR: White Cloud Press, 1999.

Islamic Groups

Ernst, Carl W. *Sufism: An Essential Introduction to the Philosophy and Practice of the Mystical Tradition of Islam*. Boston: Shambhala Publications, Inc., 1997.

Momen, Moojan. *An Introduction to Shi'i Islam: A History and Doctrines of Twelver Shi'ism*. New Haven CT: Yale University Press, 1985.

Islamic History

Armstrong, Karen. *Holy War: The Crusades and Their Impact on Today's World*. Second edition. New York: Anchor Books, 2001.
———. *Islam: A Short History*. New York: The Modern Library, 2002.
Esposito, John L., editor. *The Oxford History of Islam*. New York: Oxford University Press, 1999.
Lewis, Bernard. *Islam in History: Ideas, People, and Events in the Middle East*. Chicago: Open Court, 1993.
Maalouf, Amin. *The Crusades Through Arab Eyes*. Translated by Jon Rothschild. London: Al Saqi Books, 1984.
Williams, John Alden, editor. *Themes of Islamic Civilization*. Los Angeles: University of California Press, 1971.

Islamic law

Cook, Michael. *Commanding Right and Forbidding Wrong in Islamic Thought*. Cambridge: Cambridge University Press, 2000.
Fyzee, Asaf Ali Asghar. *Outlines of Muhammadan Law*. Third edition. London: Oxford University Press, 1964.
Qaradawi, Yusuf al-. *The Lawful and the Prohibited in Islam*. Translated by Kamal El-Hebawy, M. Moinuddin Siddiqui, and Syed Shukry. Plainfield IN: American Trust Publications, 1994.

Islam and Modernity

Berry, Donald L. *Islam and Modernity Through the Writings of Islamic Modernist Fazlur Rahman*. Lewiston NY: Edwin Mellen Press, 2003.

Lee, Robert D. *Overcoming Tradition and Modernity: The Search for Islamic Authenticity.* Boulder CO: Westview Press, 1997.

Rahman, Fazlur. *Islam and Modernity: Transformation of an Intellectual Tradition.* Chicago: University of Chicago Press, 1982.

Thompson, Michael J., editor. *Islam and the West: Critical Perspectives on Modernity.* Lanham MD: Rowman and Littlefield Publishers, Ltd., 2003.

Contemporary Islam

Algar, Hamid. *Wahhabism: A Critical Essay.* Oneonta NY: Islamic Publications International, 2002.

Cragg, Kenneth. *Counsels in Contemporary Islam.* Edinburgh: Edinburgh University Press, 1965.

Donohue, John J., and John L. Esposito, editors. *Islam in Transition: Muslim Perspectives.* New York: Oxford University Press, 1982.

Esposito, John L., and John O. Voll. *Makers of Contemporary Islam.* New York: Oxford University Press, 2001.

Haddad, Yvonne Yazbeck. *Contemporary Islam and the Challenge of History.* Albany NY: State University of New York Press, 1982.

Rahman, Fazlur. *Revival and Reform in Islam: A Study of Islamic Fundamentalism.* Edited by Ebrahim Moosa. Oxford: One World Publications, 2000.

Islam in the West

Geaves, Ron., et al., editors. *Islam and the West: Post 9/11.* Burlington VT: Ashgate Publishing Company, 2004.

Haddad, Yvonne Yazbeck, editor. *The Muslims of America.* New York: Oxford University Press, 1991.

Kepel, Gilles. *Allah in the West: Islamic Movements in America and Europe*. Translated by Susan Milner. Stanford CA: Stanford University Press, 1997.

Muslim-Christian Relations

Braswell, George W., Jr. *Islam: Its Prophet, Peoples, Politics and Power*. Nashville: Broadman and Holman Publishers, 1996.
———. *What You Need to Know about Islam and Muslims*. Nashville: Broadman and Holman Publishers, 1996.
Cragg, Kenneth. *The Call of the Minaret*. New York: Oxford University Press, 1964.
Khalidi, Tarif, editor and translator. *The Muslim Jesus: Sayings and Stories in Islamic Literature*. Cambridge MA: Harvard University Press, 2001.
Kimball, Charles. *Striving Together: A Way Forward in Christian-Muslim Relations*. Maryknoll NY: Orbis Books, 1991.
Parrinder, Geoffrey. *Jesus in the Qur'an*. New York: Oxford University Press, 1977.
Shenk, David W. *Journeys of the Muslim Nation and the Christian Church: Exploring the Mission of the Two Communities*. Scottsdale PA: Herald Press, 2003.
Van Gorder, A. Christian. *No God But God: A Path to Muslim-Christian Dialogue on God's Nature*. Maryknoll NY: Orbis Books, 2003.

INDEX

Abbasids, 62, 80-83, 85, 129
Abraham, 11-12, 14, 21, 25-26, 33, 36, 43, 50, 143, 145-146, 160
Abu Bakr, 23, 25, 58, 60, 62, 72-74, 77, 121
Abu Talib, 8, 18-19, 23, 24
Adam, 13-14, 39-42, 55, 156
al-Afghani, Jamal al-Din, 116
Afghanistan, 2, 63, 89, 91, 111-112, 126, 132, 134
A'ishah, 25, 33
Ali, 23, 49, 57-60, 62-63, 65-67, 72, 74, 77- 78, 92, 129, 143, 145, 148, 152-153
Almsgiving (See Zakat)
Angels, 38-39, 41, 43. (See also Gabriel)
Arabia, ix, xi, 1, 6-16, 17, 23, 27, 31-33, 45, 48, 55, 76, 79, 103, 137, 146-148
Arabic, x-xi, 3, 12-13, 17, 19, 35, 46-47, 80- 81, 137, 146, 151, 153
Ataturk, Mustafa Kamal, 84, 104
Ayatollah, 64, 90

Baghdad, 37, 80, 82, 147
Banu Hashim, 18, 24
Bedouin, 4, 6-9, 17, 19

Byzantine Empire, 32-33, 79, 83, 147, 150

Caliphate, 58-64, 72-85, 103, 116-117, 120- 121, 129; Rightly Guided Caliphs, 58-60, 72-78, 88-89; Umayyads, 57, 59-60, 62, 72, 76-77, 79-80, 89, 104, 129; Abbasids, 62, 80-83, 85, 129; Fatimids, 82-83; Ottomans, 83-84, 89, 101, 111
Christianity, 1, 10, 14-15, 21, 28, 32, 37, 46- 47, 56, 67, 74, 81, 85, 101, 103, 106, 108-109, 118, 121-122, 134, 146-164
Circumcision, 95, 137; Female, 138
Confession of Faith, (See Shahadah)
Community Life, 139-145
Constantinople (Istanbul), 32, 50, 79, 84, 150-151
Contemporary Issues in Islam, 102-110, 114-135; Economic Issues, 126-129; Political Issues, 120-122; Social Issues, 123-126; Theological Issues, 117-119
Cragg, Kenneth, 154, 163

Crusades, 81-82, 108, 133-134,
148-150, 154, 159, 163

David, 18, 44, 47, 146-147
Day of Judgment, 33, 40, 45,
53-54, 61, 64, 147, 156-157
Dhimmi (Monotheists
protected by Islamic Law),
94
Divorce, 7, 36, 124-125
Dome of the Rock, 14, 25-26,
79, 143
Doctrines (See Pillars of Islam)

Eating Habits, 49, 69, 95-97,
100, 143
Egypt, 2, 25, 76, 82, 89-90, 116,
132, 142, 150-151, 153

Fasting, (See Sawm)
Fatimah, 20, 23, 63, 77, 82
Fatimids, (See Caliphate,
Fatimids)
Francis (Saint) of Assisi, 150-
151

Gabriel, 13-14, 21-22, 27, 35,
38, 43, 67
al-Ghazali, Abu Hamid, 69-70,
130

Hadith, 34, 74, 82, 91, 105-106,
117, 138, 157
Hajj, 50-51, 88, 93
Hijra (Journey to Medina), x,
27-28
Husayn, 49, 65, 78, 143

Ibn Taymiyya, 115, 130-131
Ijma, 60, 63
Ijtihad, 64, 91
Imam (Immate), 61, 63-64, 66,
74, 91
India, 2-3, 63, 112, 116, 153
Infanticide, 7, 20, 137
Inheritance Laws, 7, 125, 161
Iran, 2, 63-66, 81, 111-112,
120, 153
Iraq, 2, 10, 12, 52-53, 63, 76,
78, 89, 95, 104, 120, 134,
147, 163-164
Ishmael, 11-14, 26, 50-51, 143
Islamic Community (See
Ummah)
Isma'ilis (Seveners), 63
Ithna Ashariyyah (Twelvers), 63

Jesus, 8, 15, 26, 38, 44-45, 53,
56, 118, 143,   147, 149,
155-160, 162-163
Jews, 14-15, 21, 28, 32, 44, 46,
75, 92, 102, 118, 121-122,
132, 137, 142, 146-147,
161.
Jihad, 52-53, 61, 88, 119
Jinn, 13, 39
John of Damascus, 147-148
John of Segovia, 151

Ka'ba, 10, 13-15, 20-21, 23, 25,
28, 30-32, 50, 143
Kharijites, 59, 78, 129-131, 134
Khomeini, Ayatollah, 64

Law (Islamic), (See Shariah)
Life Cycle, 136-139

Luther, Martin, 152

Mandaeans, 15
Marriage, 7, 124-125, 136, 138, 142
Martyn, Henry, 153
Mary (Mother of Jesus), 36, 44, 53, 155-156, 158-160
Massignon, Louis, 153-154
Mawdudi, Mawlana, 107
Mecca, 10-15, 17-18, 20-33, 36, 47, 50, 57-59, 72, 76-77, 81, 86-87, 89, 92-93, 108, 110, 139, 142-143, 145.
Medina, x, 10-11, 15, 17-18, 25, 27-31, 33, 36, 57, 60, 72, 76, 78, 81, 86-89, 92, 107, 142
Modernity, 99-113; Modernists, 104-105; New Religious Movements, 108-110; Revivalists, 106-108; Secularists, 103-104; Traditionalists, 105-106
Monophysite, 15, 148
Moses, 18, 22, 26, 43-45, 142-143, 146-147, 152, 156
Mu'awiya, 59, 76, 78-79, 129
Muhammad, x-xi, 6-8, 10, 14-16, 17-34, 35- 37, 43, 45-47, 50, 55, 57-63, 65-67, 72-74, 76-77, 79-80, 86-88, 92-94, 106, 109-110, 116-118, 121-122, 131, 137-138, 142-148, 151-154, 156, 159-160
Muslim Calendar, x-xi, 22, 27-28, 49-50, 142-145

Muslim-Christian Relations, 14, 28, 32, 44, 73-75, 118, 121-122, 146-164

Nation of Islam, 109-110
Nestorians, 15
North American Muslims, 111-113

Osama Bin Laden, 1, 93, 97, 112-113, 119, 132, 134
Ottoman Empire, (See Caliphate, Ottomans)

Pilgrimage, (See Hajj)
Pillars of Islam, 26, 46-52, 127
Prayer, (See Salat)
Pre-Islamic Arabia (See Arabia)
Prophets, 26, 38, 43, 46, 106, 109-110, 156

al-Qaeda, 4
Qur'an, x-xi, 3, 22-23, 25-26, 33-34, 35-56, 58, 60-61, 67-68, 77, 86-88, 91-93, 105, 108-110, 117-118, 123-124, 126-127, 137, 139-140, 144, 146-148, 151-152, 154-157, 159-160, 163

Ramadan, 49-50, 93, 95-96, 144-145
Reform Movements, 66, 70, 129-134
Rightly Guided Caliphs, (See Caliphate, Rightly Guided Caliphs)

Saladin, 82-83, 133, 149
Salat, 47-48, 50, 88, 139, 144
Satan (Shaitan) or Devil (Iblis),
    39, 41, 51
Sawm, 49-50, 93-95, 142-145
Seveners, (See Isma'ilis)
Shahadah, 46-47, 88.
Shariah, 34, 46, 56, 61, 86-98,
    115, 117-119, 122-123, 125,
    130, 139
Shi'ites, xi, 59-66, 70-71, 74,
    80-83, 89, 91-92, 95-96,
    106-108, 120-121, 138-139,
    143, 145
Sufis, 65-71, 115, 118, 130
Sunnah, 34, 58, 60, 87, 110, 118
Sunnis, 60-66, 70-71, 77, 106,
    108, 120-121

Turkey, 2, 32, 50, 63, 82, 84,
    89, 104, 116
Twelvers, (See Ithna
    Ashariyyah)

Ulama, 60, 90-91, 120
Umar, 58, 62, 74-76
Umayyads, (See Caliphate,
    Umayyads)
Ummah, 26, 28-30, 32-33, 38,
    42-43, 47, 49, 51-53, 55,
    57-63, 69, 72-77, 82, 86-88,
    90-94, 97, 100, 103-104,
    107, 114-115, 118-121, 123,
    127, 129-130, 132, 135,
    139-145
Uthman, 59, 62, 76-78

Wahhabism, 115-116, 130, 132
Women, 36, 49, 51, 93, 105,
    123-126, 138, 141-142; In
    Pre-Islamic Arabia, 7, 17

Zakat, 48-49, 58, 88, 92-94,
    127-128
Zaydis, 63
Zoroastrianism, 16, 75